chrismukkah

Everything You Need to Know to Celebrate the Hybrid Holiday

HOW TO WRAP

chriʃmukkah

by RON GOMPERTZ

...will
..., and
...e effect.

STEWART, TABORI & CHANG / NEW YORK

RIGI

It's easy when you know how.
Always begin by clearing a tabletop
and assembling all
the needed materials—
scissors, paper, ribbon, tape, labels.
Then, from the inside out,
here's how:

Miter ends, ... *, and tape
them shut. (In... ually, there's a*

*Now tie the loops together tightly
around the center—instant bow!
Your creation is ready to be tied or
taped securely in place. (If you
want to make really fancy bows,
send 25¢ to Chicago Printed String,
2300 Logan Blvd., Chicago 47, Illi-*

So, what's it going to be?
Fruitcake or potato latkes?
Spin the dreidel or get kissed
under the mistletoe?
Switch on the tree or strike
a match to the menorah?
Sing "Rock of Ages" or
"Jingle Bell Rock"?

Now you don't have to choose.
This book is for both
Christians and Jews.
Here you can have it all.
Here we celebrate Chrismukkah!

Dedicated to my merry mish-mash family: Michelle, Minna Meadow, and NaNa Rita.

In memory of my father, Fred, a dreamer and eternal optimist and my grandmothers, Oma Betty and Omi Friedel, whose matzo balls were always filled with love.

CONTENTS

For You... A Little Chrismukkah!

"And if Hanukkah Harry is helping Santa, maybe that means that Christians and Jews, deep down, are pretty much the same. Maybe that's the true meaning of Christmas!"

—Saturday Night Live skit (12/16/89)

WE'RE CELEBRATING THE HOLIDAYS TOGETHER?

"When Mel [Brooks] told his Jewish mother he was marrying an Italian girl, she said, 'Bring her over. I'll be in the kitchen… with my head in the oven."

—ANNE BANCROFT

CHRISMUKKAH (KRIS-muh-kuh) *n.* A hybrid holiday celebration that merges elements of both Christmas and Hanukkah. Most often observed by families with part or full Jewish and Christian members.

Okay, I need to admit something up front: Chrismukkah is pretend. It doesn't exist. It's made up. Wishful thinking. A hoax holiday.

I confess, you won't find Chrismukkah on the calendar. Observing it won't earn you extra days off from work or school. Chrismukkah won't bring you spiritual enlightenment, or get you right with God. Your rabbi or priest won't know much about it, and if you ask your parents, they may wonder what they did wrong to deserve this.

Nonetheless, for the growing number of interfaith families whose living rooms sport both a menorah and a tree, Chrismukkah is a good solution to the so-called "December Dilemma." For we intermarried folk, Chrismukkah is a "merry mish-mash" season every bit as real as Santa Claus, Hanukkah Harry and the notion of "peace on earth and good will toward man."

Chrismukkah begins on the first night of Hanukkah and continues through Christmas Day or the last night of Hanukkah, whichever occurs later. Depending on the year, it can last between eight and thirty days.

Chrismukkah is a celebration of diversity, a global gumbo of cherished secular traditions. It's the good stuff we all enjoy, no matter what our religion: sleigh bells, eggnog, snowmen, twinkling

lights, flickering candles, exchanging gifts with family and friends. It's a medley of Bing Crosby's "Chestnuts Roasting on an Open Fire," Alvin and the Chipmunks' "Christmas Don't Be Late," Irving Berlin's "White Christmas," and Adam Sandler's nebbish-y "The Hanukkah Song." It's decorating the tree with bagels and candy canes, snacking on gingerbread dreidels and nibbling chocolate gelt. It's cooking up hybrid holiday recipes like cranberry sweet potato latkes, kosher fruitcake and "matza" pizza.

If you're a parent whose spouse celebrates the "other" holiday, you surely appreciate Chrismukkah's appeal. What kid wouldn't love the idea of a super stretched-out holiday combining the best of both Hanukkah and Christmas? Eight days of gifts plus one day of many gifts!

THE CHRISMUKKAH CONVERSION

The first flurries of winter were already in the air and our wedding day was just a few months away. When the phone rang, I recognized the number and let it go through to voice mail. My fiancée

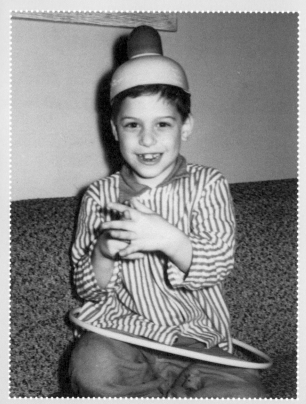

Michelle had cautioned me to expect the call from her parents. It was an invitation that couldn't easily be turned down.

In my experience, the true meaning of Christmas was getting some time away from work. With our baby on the way, I had planned to surprise Michelle with a Hawaiian vacation. There would be no time for a traditional honeymoon later. But to Michelle, Christmas signaled the annual pilgrimage home to Indiana to visit the family. My Christmas future was clear. It was far more likely I'd be spending the holidays sitting at my in-laws' kitchen island than at the tiki bar on a tropical island. Even though Michelle was not religious, the family I was marrying into took Christmas very seriously. I knew this would take some getting used to—even for a liberal-minded Jewish person like me.

HEBREW HOOSIER HOLIDAY

We picked up the keys to the rental car at the Avis kiosk on Christmas Eve afternoon. During the drive from the Indy airport, I kept losing my bearings. The flat Midwestern landscape was missing any natural landmarks to use as reference points... and at the time, this seemed metaphorical. Michelle's father had been a pastor with the United Church of Christ for most of his career, and her mother was the "church lady." Michelle's brother was a deacon, and even though I didn't know exactly what a deacon did, all this Christianity made me nervous.

As we pulled into the driveway of the tidy, red brick house on Shady Lane, the front door opened to reveal a gaggle of children waiting to see Auntie

Michelle and their new uncle-to-be. Behind the kids, several rows of near in-laws stood smiling, watching us unload our bags. I'd tried to memorize everyone's name on the flight in, but now my mind was mostly blank. Nadine, Michelle's mother, hugged me politely, patting me on the back. "Nice to see you." She was trim, pale, with short-cropped white hair, and reminded me of David Letterman's mother, who just happened to belong to the same church. Michelle's father, John, looked a little like Bob Newhart, and he welcomed me with a warm handshake. In a blur, I met the rest of the family, after which everyone returned to their holiday responsibilities. The women gathered in the kitchen, busy with the meal; the men sat in the den, watching highlights of some big game. Stereotyping Christians, I had expected lots of yuletide indulgence, but my hopes of getting shnockered on eggnog and brandy fizzled when I learned this was an alcohol-free family. Oy! It was going to be a long week.

Thankfully, there was food aplenty: chips and dips, Christmas cookies, Rice Krispies® Treats, green bean casserole, Chex® Mix, lemonade and cans of "pop." The children lay on the living room floor, mesmerized by a Barney video. When we sat down for Christmas dinner, it was still light out and seemed too early for a civilized meal. I had a brief moment of panic, thinking of Ben Stiller mangling grace in Meet the Parents. In a pinch I could always recite the Hanukkah Bruchah. Thankfully John handled the blessings.

Platters were passed around, piled high with Christmas turkey, sweet potatoes and mixed vegetables. I could get used to this! Compliments were dished out as quickly as the food: "Nadine, I must get your cranberry tart recipe." The conversation revolved around adorable things the children had said and done, followed by the church health report. Everyone was very sincere. There were no embarrassing outbursts. No one talked while chewing. There were long pauses between each sentence.

I was really starting to miss my own family. Our meals were unruly boisterous affairs. We didn't wait for plates to be passed; we reached across the table. Arguing was encouraged; it seemed rude to let anyone finish a sentence and interrupting was a sign of respect. Religion, politics and embarrassing personal tidbits were the stuff of good conversation. Sarcasm was an art form. Pounding on the table with fists, a good way to emphasize a point.

"Ron, how is your family spending the Christmas holiday?" Aunt Jean asked me from across the table, out of the blue.

I was momentarily startled. I assumed everyone knew I was Jewish, and I didn't know how to address the question. I finished chewing my mincemeat pie, not daring to talk with my mouth full. "Umm, my family doesn't usually get together this time of year." I said tentatively, aware that all eyes were on me. "For most Jewish people, Hanukkah is not a major religious holiday. It's not like Christmas... for that we have Passover and Yom Kippur."

Michelle saved me from rambling into off-limits material, "Ron taught me how to light the Hanukkah menorah," she interjected diplomatically.

"Oh, isn't that nice?" Aunt Jean said.

That was the end of my inquisition. No more personal questions were asked. After dessert, we all drove over to Saint Peter's Church for the 7 PM Christmas Eve candlelight service.

BORN AGAIN

I sat in the wooden pew between Michelle, her parents and a few hundred Hoosier worshippers. The choir sang their hearts out. The carols were lovely and familiar, those Christmas songs that stick in your head like caramel in teeth, until you floss them out in January. Whenever the pastor mentioned "Jesus," which was often, I could feel my cheeks getting hot. I became increasingly self-conscious of my Jewish-ness. It was obvious to all I didn't belong. A spotlight shone from above, focusing on my above-average-sized nose. From my clean-shaven face, a dark beard grew long and unkempt. Hasidic pais dropped in ringlets past my cheeks. A Christmas angel, young and Woody

Allen-ish, hovered behind me, nervously flapping his wings while trying to drop a red and green yarmulke on my skull, whispering stale old lines from *Annie Hall* into my ear. "I would never join any club that would have me for a member," he hissed.

The room began to spin. I was ready to evacuate in panic when Michelle reached over and squeezed my hand, unaware of my inner turmoil. She leaned over and whispered, "Thanks for coming here with me. It means a lot."

I put my arm around my wife-to-be's shoulder and remembered how good-natured she had been during Hanukkah, learning the Hebrew blessings and helping me light the menorah each night; her brave attempts at making latkes and chicken matzo ball soup. I settled back and relaxed.

When the service was over, everyone lined up to shake hands with the pastor. I wished him a "Merry Christmas," feeling a little odd, and half expecting a bolt of lightening to strike me down as I exited the church. As we walked into the parking lot, a fresh blanket of snow covered all the cars. I had an epiphany of sorts. I felt a renewed sense of confidence in my own identity as a Jew. I thought about my mother and everything she had gone through.

WEIHNUKKAH

When I was growing up, we had a Hanukkah bush. It was decorated with paper stars, dreidel ornaments, candy canes and red mesh Santa stockings. It was my mother's tradition. She had grown up with one Jewish and one Christian parent in Germany. She fondly remembered celebrating both her father's Christmas (*Weihnachten*) and her mother's Hanukkah before things got bad. The secular, assimilated Jews of pre-Nazi Germany had an ironic name to describe their mix of holiday traditions—"Weihnukkah." It translates into English as "Chrismukkah."

By the time my mother was eight years old, Hitler made it impossible for her family to celebrate any holiday. She was lucky to survive and eventually found her way to America, where she met my father. For Mom, the holidays were always accompanied by bittersweet memories. Looking back, I now better appreciate how important our "Weihnukkah" bush was to my mother.

AND THEN THERE WAS CHRISMUKKAH

Michelle and I married soon after our first Christmas visit to Indiana together. Not long after, our daughter Minna, was born. The idea for a Web site catering to mish-mash families came to us during that early magical time of being parents. With the Jewish Gentile intermarriage rate approaching 50 percent, we hoped to have an appreciative audience. We launched Chrismukkah.com ... and the rest is history.

Like most interfaith couples, neither Michelle nor I have any interest in converting to the other's faith. While we are not religious, we are both proud of our cultural heritage. At the same time, we are curious to learn about, and happy to help each other celebrate our respective traditions and customs. Some people might (and do) caution, "You can't have it both ways. Keep the holidays separate. Don't confuse your children." Yet we are determined to respect and honor our traditions, while acknowledging our new combination family. Most importantly, we want Minna to grow up informed, tolerant and balanced.

As a multicultural family, we are part of a growing demographic trend in America that is a by-product of our country's melting-pot history. From this perspective, Chrismukkah is more than just a pretend holiday about two incompatible religions. Viewing things in the long-range context of a timeline, Chrismukkah is part of an evolutionary continuum as old as Judaism and Christianity.

Now, when the holidays come around each year, I look forward to our family trip back to Indiana to spend Christmas... and Michelle looks forward to celebrating Hanukkah at our house. This is the spirit of Chrismukkah.

One day, Minna may come running home from school, tears in her eyes, taunted by friends who say there is no such thing as Santa Claus or the Hanukkah Man. If that day comes, I will sit her down, tell her the story of our mish-mash family and reassure her, saying, "Yes, Minna, there really is a Chrismukkah."

CORPORATE MERGER ANNOUNCED

"Continuing the current trend of large-scale mergers and acquisitions, it was announced today at a press conference that Christmas and Hanukkah will merge. An industry source said that the deal had been in the works for about 1,300 years. While details were not available at press time, it is believed that the overhead cost of having twelve days of Christmas and eight days of Hanukkah was becoming prohibitive for both sides. By combining forces, we're told, the world will be able to enjoy consistently high-quality service during the Fifteen Days of Chrismukkah, as the new holiday is being called.

Massive layoffs are expected, with lords a-leaping and maids a-milking being the hardest hit. As part of the conditions of the agreement, the letters on the dreidel, currently in Hebrew, will be replaced by Latin, thus becoming unintelligible to a wider audience. Also, instead of translating to "A great miracle happened there" the message on the dreidel will be the more populist "Miraculous shit happens." In exchange, it is believed that Hanukkah Harry will be allowed to use Santa Claus' vast merchandising resources for buying and delivering gifts.

One of the sticking points holding up the agreement for at least three hundred years was the question of whether Jewish children could leave milk and cookies for Santa even after having eaten meat for dinner. A breakthrough came last year, when Oreos were finally declared to be Kosher. All sides appeared happy about this.

A spokesman for Christmas, Inc., declined to say whether a takeover of Kwanzaa might not be in the works as well. He merely pointed out that, were it not for the independent existence of Kwanzaa, the merger between Christmas and Hanukkah might indeed be seen as an unfair cornering of the holiday market. Fortunately for all concerned, he said, Kwanzaa will help to maintain the competitive balance.

He then closed the press conference by leading all present in a rousing rendition of 'Oy Vey, All Ye Faithful.'"

The original "Chrismukkah" spoof press release, written by Michael Nathanson.

The Chrismukkah Timeline

1400 BCE

Pyramid slave laborer delivers first one-liner:
"When Moses was born, his mother sent him off
on a Mediterranean cruise… but he was in
de Nile."

1360 BCE

First mixed marriage occurs when Moses gets
hitched to Zipporah, daughter of the high priest
of a nomadic Arabian tribe.

1000 BCE

Wild and crazy winter solstice celebration held
in ancient Greece. "Lenaia: The Festival of Wild
Women," involves frenzied dancing. Then the
women hook up with a man, chop him to pieces
and eat him.

596 BCE

The Buddha achieves enlightenment. Soon after,
Zen-Judaism proclaims, "Be patient and achieve
all things. Be impatient and achieve all things
faster."

250 BCE

More winter solstice celebrations ensue, with
saturnalia getting a little kinky. After too
much eggnog, Romans parade around naked
carrying candles and cross-dressing. Masters
pretend to be slaves and slaves pretend to be
masters.

167 BCE

Syrian King Antiochus outlaws Judaism in Jerusalem. After a three-year battle, the Jewish Maccabees (led by Judah, "the Hammer") are victorious. On the twenty-fifth day of the Hebrew month of Kislev, a reception is held to re-dedicate the temple, but the caterer forgets the oil. A small amount is scrounged, and miraculously burns for eight days, until new supplies arrive from Zabar's. Hanukkah is born.

6 BCE

The Virgin Mary gives birth to Jesus. Like any Jewish mother, she thinks her son is a gift from God.

50 CE

Graffiti found on bathroom wall of Bethlehem Jewish Theological Seminary: "Jesus was only half Jewish. The good news is, it was on his mother's side."

270 CE

The historic inspiration for Santa Claus, Saint Nicholas of Myra, is born in Turkey.

364 CE

Church officials, fed up with pagan debauchery (see saturnalia), promote a fledgling Christmas holiday on December 25. Christianity soon becomes the official Roman faith. By popular demand, Christmas assumes most of the old rituals of saturnalia, minus the nudity.

1184–1834

The Inquisition is established by the Catholic Church to suppress heresy and force baptisms of non-Christians. Millions die during its 700-year reign.

1492
Columbus discovers America, by mistake.

1570
A small fir tree is decorated with apples and cheese for Christmas in Germany.

1614
The Dutch buy Manhattan from local Indians for sixty guilders ($24). They pay wholesale.

1615
Dutchman Jan Macy opens a bead-and-trinket stand on Herald Square and dresses up as "Sinterklaas" to woo customers from Gimbel's.

1659
Christmas outlawed in Massachusetts for being "highly dishonorable to the name of Christ." The ban lasts more than twenty years.

1791
The First Amendment to the U.S. Constitution guarantees freedom of religion and requires a wall of separation between church and state.

1830
Tree decorating fad is introduced to America by German immigrants.

1870
Congress makes Christmas a federal holiday to give Jewish children two weeks off from school to ponder the meaning of separation of church and state.

1880
Jews in Germany celebrate Hanukkah in much the same way Christians celebrate Weihnachten (Christmas), by decorating trees and baking cookies. The new hybrid holiday "Weihnukkah" is subtitled "the festival of the world around us."

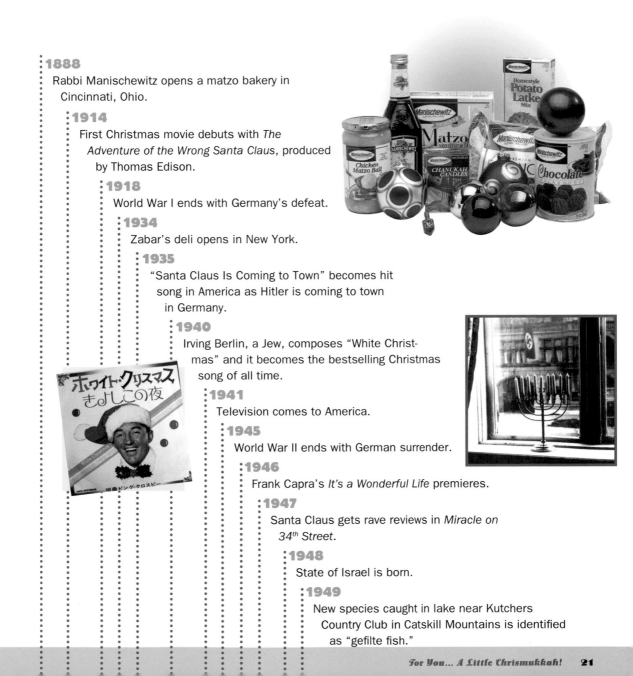

1888
Rabbi Manischewitz opens a matzo bakery in
Cincinnati, Ohio.

1914
First Christmas movie debuts with *The
Adventure of the Wrong Santa Claus*, produced
by Thomas Edison.

1918
World War I ends with Germany's defeat.

1934
Zabar's deli opens in New York.

1935
"Santa Claus Is Coming to Town" becomes hit
song in America as Hitler is coming to town
in Germany.

1940
Irving Berlin, a Jew, composes "White Christmas" and it becomes the bestselling Christmas
song of all time.

1941
Television comes to America.

1945
World War II ends with German surrender.

1946
Frank Capra's *It's a Wonderful Life* premieres.

1947
Santa Claus gets rave reviews in *Miracle on
34th Street*.

1948
State of Israel is born.

1949
New species caught in lake near Kutchers
Country Club in Catskill Mountains is identified
as "gefilte fish."

1949
"Rudolph the Red Nosed Reindeer" is huge hit for Gene Autry.

1950
"Frosty the Snowman" is huge follow-up hit for Gene Autry.

1951
Lenny Bruce (formerly Leonard Schneider) is arrested in Miami for impersonating a priest soliciting donations for a leper colony run by the Brother Mathias Foundation in British Guiana.

1953
Color television broadcasting begins. *The Goldbergs* is first television show with Jews as principal characters.

1955
Civil Rights movement begins.

1956
"Hanukkah Bush" and "Hanukkah Man" become popular in Jewish homes.

1962
The Beatles are discovered by Jewish record-store owner Brian Epstein.

1965
Counter-culture, peace protest era begins.

1966
Kwanzaa, an African-American cultural holiday, is conceived by Dr. Maulana Ron Karenga.

1966
"The Grinch Who Stole Christmas" appears on television: "Every Who Down in Who-ville Liked Christmas a lot… But the Grinch, Who lived just north of Who-ville, Did NOT!"

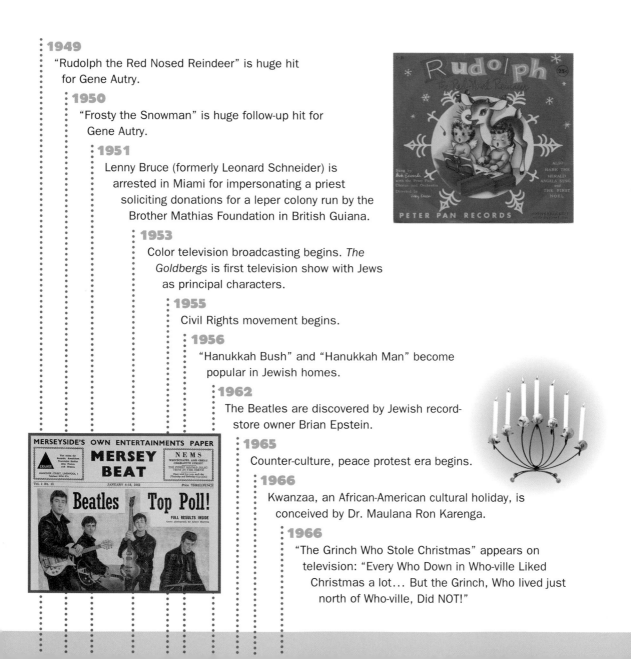

1969
The dove, a common symbol of the holy spirit in
Christianity, becomes an icon of the peace move-
ment when it is used in the logo for Woodstock,
a massive music festival organized by four
Jewish hippies.

1971
John and Yoko release *Imagine* and *Happy Xmas
(War is Over)*.

1970–1979
Jewish intermarriage rate more than doubles
during this decade, to 28 percent. Tradition of
parents sitting shiva for children who intermarry
wanes.

1972
Chrismukkah Golden Years begins with *Bridget
Loves Bernie*: first prime-time television show to
feature Jewish-Christian intermarried couple.

1979
Bob (Zimmerman) Dylan is born again as
a Christian.

1987
More Chrismukkah television with *Thirtysome-
thing*, featuring interfaith couple.

1989
The quintessential New York Jewish sitcom *Seinfeld* hits the airwaves.

1989
"Hanukkah Harry" appears on the small screen,
played by Jon Lovitz in a *Saturday Night
Live* skit.

1990
Jewish intermarriage rate reaches 43 percent.

1992

Jennifer Bleyer's short-lived Jewish punk 'zine, *Mazel Tov Cocktail*, ushers in era of cool Jew websites and magazines like *Jewhoo*, *Jewlicious*, *Jewcy*, *Jew School* and *Heeb*.

1996

Adam Sandler releases "The Hanukkah Song."

1996

Jewish intermarriage rate hits 47 percent.

1997

Festivus holiday introduced on *Seinfeld* episode "The Strike."

MODERN CHRISMUKKAH ERA BEGINS

12/1/98

High school teacher Michael Nathanson sends out fake press release about the corporate merger of Christmas and Hanukkah.

3/27/99

The Honolulu Star-Bulletin quotes a Jewish man marrying a Christian woman: "I want to give our children the best of both worlds. We'll have Hanukkah and we'll have Christmas and a Chrismukkah tree."

12/1/99

"A Lonely Jew on Christmas" song becomes instant classic on *South Park*'s "Mr. Hankey's Christmas" episode.

5/15/03

Minna Meadow Gompertz is born, inspiring launch of www.chrismukkah.com.

7/8/03

Charlotte York converts to Judaism on *Sex and the City*.

12/3/03
"The Best Chrismukkah Ever" episode airs on Fox soap *The O.C.*, giving Chrismukkah mainstream exposure.

12/5/03
First Chrismukkah cards are mailed.

12/19/03
The Hebrew Hammer movie is released.

8/15/04
Madonna announces she is the "Messiah of Kabbalah."

12/1/04
Virgin Mobile announces "Chrismahanukwanzakah" TV ad campaign.

12/6/04
New York Catholic League denounces Chrismukkah in press release.

12/15/04
Edinburgh Scotsman reports "Chrismukkah" added to the *Chambers Dictionary* of Scotland.

12/27/04
Time magazine declares "Chrismukkah" a buzzword of the year.

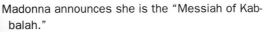

10/28/05
The Jewish Museum of Berlin opens the exhibition, Chrismukkah: Stories of Christmas and Hanukkah.

11/7/05
Chrismukkah: The Merry Mish-Mash Holiday Cookbook is released.

12/05
National media picks up on Chrismukkah craze. Featured on the *Today Show*, in *USA Today*, *The New York Times*, the *L.A. Times*, *The Wall Street Journal* and elsewhere.

Tradition, Tradition!

*"You may ask,
'How did this tradition get started?'
I'll tell you.
I don't know.
But it's a tradition!"*

—TEVYE IN *FIDDLER ON THE ROOF*

Christmas and Hanukkah are all about tradition. Tradition is why they are cherished and how they are celebrated. Both holidays share many memories: fanciful store window displays, lighting of lights, delicious foods, gaining five pounds in a week, shmaltzy old songs, sappy holiday movies, vapid variety specials on television, gleefully unwrapping presents, disappointment at seeing what's inside, gathering with relatives, fighting with relatives, and best of all, from a kid's perspective, getting a few weeks off from school!

Most of these holiday traditions are so familiar that no one questions them. Christmas and Hanukkah each go back more than 2,000 years, and to paraphrase *Fiddler on the Roof*, I don't have a clue how these traditions got started.

Who put Santa on the roof, when he could have easily left the gifts on the front porch? Why are Christmas trees northern evergreens rather than fruit trees native to Bethlehem? Why does Hanukkah stretch for eight days instead of one and why in God's name do you spin a dreidel? How come people kiss under the mistletoe? And what's with the carolers? I don't know, but it's a tradition!

Thankfully, those who choose to celebrate Chrismukkah won't have to grapple with these perplexing questions. As a brand-new, twenty-first-century pseudoholiday, Chrismukkah is more connected to postmodern pop-culture traditions than the ancient ones. One of the coolest things about Chrismukkah is its flexibility to be mixed and matched to your own personal specifications and preferences. As a totally secular neoholiday, there are no religious rules to execrate, no rituals to ignore, no icons to blaspheme, no dogma, nothing to constrain your celebration. How you choose to observe Chrismukkah is entirely up to you.

Nonetheless, before heading forth blissfully into the merry mish-mash world of Chrismukkah, let's do one final review of the quaint old-school traditions you've probably forgotten about since graduating (or dropping out) of Sunday school or Hebrew school.

WINTER SOLSTICE was the common denominator for many of the world's religions. The solstice falls on or about December 21, the shortest day of the year and the time when the sun is at its weakest. Before they understood the seasonal cycles, ancient people had conniptions worrying that the world was headed toward permanent darkness and cold. Ancient solstice celebrations like yule and saturnalia celebrated the extreme joy everyone felt as they realized the sun, and warmer days, would soon be returning.

Yule was a popular Winter Solstice festival celebrated by Germanic pre-Christian tribes in Northern Europe. Many of the modern rituals associated with Christmas, such as burning a Yule log, eating ham and hanging boughs of holly, came from yule.

SATURNALIA was the major winter holiday of the Roman Empire. Saturnalia was all about worshipping Saturn, the harvest god, and Mithras, the god of light. It was a joyous week-long celebration and everyone shared special saturnalia meals, decorated their homes with evergreen trees, holly and mistletoe, exchanged gifts, and paraded around town in groups carrying candles and singing saturnalia songs. Sound familiar? When the Christian church came to power in the third century, Christmas became the new official holiday of the Roman Empire. They scheduled it to overlap saturnalia like an eclipse of the sun. Then, to please the masses, the favorite rituals of saturnalia were adopted by Christmas. It wasn't long before most had forgotten about the old pagan holiday.

CHRISTMAS began as an obscure little holiday to celebrate the birth of a Jewish guy named Jesus. Who knew what a big deal it would become? After exhaustive research, I still couldn't pin down the actual date of Jesus' birth. Somewhere in May of 7 B.C.E. many scholars believe. But the Church decided to make the official birthday December 25, perhaps to give everybody a long week off through New Year's. For a few decades in the late 1600s, Christmas was outlawed in England and parts of America because of its pagan rituals.

BOXING DAY is celebrated on December 26 in Canada, Great Britain, Australia and South Africa by giving gifts and donations to the poor and needy.

SANTA CLAUS is the American franchise of the multinational conglomerate known as Saint Nicholas and Company. Like Chrismukkah, Santa is also a mish-mash product of the melting pot, a pastiche of mythical folk heroes from around the world, some of them older than Christmas itself. Santa's ancestral relatives include:

• *Saint Nicholas of Myra*, the Chairman of the Board of Saint Nicholas and Company.

• *Sinterklaas*, the Dutch guy who nearly sued Santa Claus for copyright infringement.

• *Odin*, the one-eyed god who leaves candy in exchange for hay for his flying horses.

• *Yule Goat*, who delivers presents on Christmas Eve in northern Europe.

• *Tomten*, the cute Scandinavian gnome with the red hat and white beard.

• *Krampus*, the German imp who resembles a cross between Satan and Rumpelstiltzkin.

• *Father Christmas*, the regal Brit who typically wears a green fur-lined robe.

• *Papa Noel*, the Spanish delivery guy who climbs balconies rather than chimneys.

• *Father Frost*, the Ukrainian hero who delivers gifts with the help of Snowflake Girl.

• The Australian *Father Christmas*, whose sled is pulled by kangaroos.

• *La Befana*, the Italian good witch who flies around with presents on her broomstick.

America's Santa Claus was first documented during the 1700s. In those days he was a tall, thin man who wore a bishop's robe and rode a white horse. By 1809, he had put on weight, becoming to be described as a stout man wearing a big hat, oversized pants and smoking a long pipe. Santa rode over the treetops in a wagon filled with presents.

En glad Jul!

340

Joyeux Noël
aux enfants sages

GOTT NYTT ÅR

REINDEER TRIVIA

• **More than five million reindeer live in Scandinavia, Russia, Greenland, Canada, and Alaska.**

• **Male reindeer shed their antlers in the fall, while female reindeer keep theirs until spring. This invites speculation about Rudolph's true gender identity.**

• **Dunder and Blixem changed their names to Donner and Blitzen.**

• **Siberian Shaman believe reindeer actually do fly.**

• **Reindeer are also known as "Tundra Cows."**

A few decades later, the poem "'Twas the Night before Christmas" described Santa as a jolly man with twinkling eyes and a red nose. In the story, he wore a suit trimmed with white fur and traveled in a sleigh pulled by eight reindeer.

During the Civil War, cartoons in *Harper's Weekly* were the first to depict Santa in his North Pole workshop. During the 1930s, the Coca-Cola company, looking for ways to increase their slow winter sales, used Santa for an advertising campaign showing him drinking Coca-Cola. The Santa-Coke partnership caused rumors that Coca-Cola actually invented Santa Claus.

RUDOLPH THE RED-NOSED REINDEER was invented as a gimmick for the department store Montgomery Ward. In 1939, one of their copy-writers was instructed to write a Christmas story that would have wide appeal. Borrowing elements from "The Ugly Duckling," Robert May wrote of an underdog reindeer ostracized by his herd because of a physical defect: a glowing red nose.

May's boss nearly rejected the story, worrying that the red nose would conjure up an image of a drunkard. But Rudolph's red nose got the green light, and more than six million copies of the story were given away to shoppers.

In 1948, May asked his brother-in-law, song-writer Johnny Marks, to come up with a melody and lyrics. They pitched the new Rudolph song to Gene Autry and within a year, it had become a bestselling Christmas song of all time, second only to "White Christmas." Rudolph movies and television shows followed.

FROSTY THE SNOWMAN is a baby boomer, born in 1950 to songwriting team Jack Rollins and Steve Nelson. With his decidedly square corn cob pipe and button nose, Frosty arrived just before the dawn of rock and roll. Hoping to make some cold cash with a follow-up hit to "Rudolph," Gene Autry agreed to record the song. Everyone involved got a blizzard that year.

DECKING THE HALLS goes way back to pagan times, when people gathered evergreen trees, ivy, rosemary, bay, laurel, and anything else that stayed green during the winter. All were symbols of everlasting life and, during the short, dark days, were meant to ensure the return of vegetation in the spring.

THE CHRISTMAS TREE origin is difficult to pin down. Decorating the home with pine trees originated with saturnalia. Many still believe that ever-greens and decorations should never be put up prior to Christmas Eve for fear of attracting evil spirits.

ORNAMENTS were first used to decorate trees in Germany more than 500 years ago. Ornaments were typically made from fruit, cookies and candy. F. W. Woolworth introduced glass ornaments to America in 1890 when he imported them after seeing them on a trip to Germany.

TINSEL became popular after a story circulated that a poor German woman's tree had became infested with spiders, and the Christ Child turned the webs into silver.

CANDLES were first lit during a pagan midwinter festival called "Candlemas." The candles were lit for sanitary reasons—by midwinter, homes had become filthy with soot and dirt, and people cleaned their houses by candlelight. The early Catholic

Church liked the idea and adopted the practice to commemorate Jesus' birth.

ELECTRIC LIGHTS were first switched on in 1882 by a colleague of Thomas Edison. Since electric lights weren't flammable like candles, they quickly became popular. Decorating the outside of homes with strings of multicolored lights became popular early in the 1900s when electricity became more readily available.

WREATHS began as a cloth band tied around one's head like a sweatband. During the Olympic games in Greece, each host city awarded head garlands made of branches of local trees to the winning athletes. Decorative wreaths became very common after this.

HOLLY and **MISTLETOE** were considered magical and used to ward off witches, lightning and infertility. Consequently many people liked to hang them in the house year round. According to the rules of tradition, a man may only kiss a girl under a sprig of mistletoe if he plucks a berry from the plant with each kiss. Once the berries are gone, so is the kissing.

POINSETTIA was named after Joel Poinsett, an American ambassador to Mexico. In 1829 Poinsett sent some home to South Carolina for his greenhouse. He'd been intrigued after hearing the legend about the flower—story has it that a poor child gathered weeds into the form of a bouquet to give as a gift to Christ. When he approached the altar in a church, the bouquet suddenly transformed into brilliant red blooms.

ANGELS date back to Roman times but have somewhat fallen from grace since their heyday in the Middle Ages. Angels remain popular as Christmas tree toppers, lawn ornaments and on wedding invites. And don't forget the starring role they play in *It's a Wonderful Life.*

CHRISTMAS STOCKINGS originated with a story about the generous Saint Nicholas of Myra once tossing three coins down the chimney of a home where three poor sisters lived. One coin fell into each of three stockings the girls had left drying by the fireplace.

Quickest
Fruitcake
ever!
You start with
Betty Crocker
Date Bar
Mix

CANDY CANES may seem like simple sweets, but lore has it they were invented by a candy maker in Indiana who wanted the stripes to represent Christ's white purity and red blood, and the shape to represent the letter "J". This story is a good example of how formerly secular holiday traditions can become infused with religious meaning well after the fact: Sugarcane candies were popular in Europe long before there was an Indiana. The bent candy cane dates back to Germany around 1670.

GINGERBREAD was originally a solid block of honey, baked with flour, ginger, breadcrumbs and spices, popular in medieval England. Gradually, gingerbread became more cakelike, often decorated and given as gifts, much like a box of chocolates is given today. The tradition of forming gingerbread into houses, castles and biblical scenes became popular in the eighteenth century.

FRUITCAKE has been a part of festive celebrations since Roman times, when cooks mixed raisins, pine nuts and pomegranate seeds into barley mash. Fruitcake was considered semisacred in parts of Europe where it was illegal to make one outside of Christmas or Easter.

HOW TO MAKE A SNOWMAN

- The ideal time to make a snowman is when the temperature is in the mid-thirties and the snow is not too dry or slushy. Be sure to wear waterproof gloves.

- Pack several handfuls of snow together into a solid ball. Roll the ball around on the snow. Be sure to keep the ball round as best you can. Position this ball—the bottom of the snowman—where you want it.

- Make a slightly smaller ball for the body using the same roll around-on-the-snow method as described above. Flatten the bottom ball and place the second ball on top of it.

- Make the smallest ball for the head, using the method described above. Flatten the middle ball and place the head on top of it.

- Pack snow into the joints between balls to stabilize them.

- Stick one branch on each side of middle ball, forming two arms.

- To the face, add eyes, nose and mouth with carrot, raisins, pebbles or charcoal.

- Dress up snowman in scarf, hat and pipe.

MINCEMEAT PIES are meant to bring good luck. According to tradition, one should eat as many whole pies as possible on Christmas Day, each at a different person's house. However, it's considered bad luck to cut a mincemeat pie or to eat one before Christmas Eve.

CHRISTMAS PUDDING should always be stirred at least three times by each member of the family. A coin, a thimble and a ring should be tossed into the mix. The person who finds the coin will be lucky, the thimble, wealthy, and the ring, lucky in love.

CHRISTMAS CARDS are a relatively recent invention. The first card was printed by an Englishman in 1843. It said "A Merry Christmas and a Happy New Year to you." Two billion Christmas cards are sent each year. Today, Hallmark reports their best selling card is "A Merry Christmas and a Happy New Year to you."

CHRISTMAS GIFT GIVING is the economic engine that drives American retailing. Christmas sales represent 30 percent of total annual sales for many stores. In the pagan days of saturnalia, people gave simple gifts of pine branches, evergreen wreaths, a jar of incense or a candle to honor the god Zeus. If that tradition were to catch on again, big-box retailers might soon become Wailing Wall marts.

CAROLING is another tradition that began with saturnalia. It's important to know that if carolers drop by, no matter how off key they sing, tradition dictates you should always offer food, beverage or money. Also know that it's considered unlucky to sing Christmas carols outside the Christmas season. I'm sure you'll agree that is a good superstition.

Santa Shmanta vs. Hanukkah Harry

SANTA CLAUS EXTREME MAKEOVER

The Claus persona, an out-of-shape, suspiciously jolly, white Anglo-Saxon patriarch, seems like an anachronism in a postmodern world of geopolitical complexity, cultural diversity and body-health consciousness.

No matter how sincere Santa's merry motives may be, his message "Be good for goodness' sake" has been undermined by his own willingness to be co-opted, exploited and crassly commercialized. Nick's saintly reputation has been compromised by overexposure in the malls and magazines, his credibility bought and paid for by corporations and big-box retailers. Santa is long overdue for an "Extreme Makeover: Chrismukkah Edition." With our casting call for alternative Santa types, we aim to put the "cool" back in yule.

GODZILLA CLAUS (KING OF THE KRINGLES.)

BEAR CLAUS (WHO COULD RESIST? CUTE, CUDDLY AND SWEET TO EAT.)

ROBO CLAUS (JOLLY 3CPO, ASTROBOY, GORT AND ROBBY SAVE THE FUTURE.)

TROLL CLAUS (THE WILD YELLOW-HAIRED FELLOW IS A KITCHMUKKAH KLASSIC.)

YAMA CLAUS (TRADE IN THE OLD FLEECE HAT FOR A RED AND GREEN SATIN YARMULKE.)

BARBIE CLAUS (NOT TO BE CONFUSED WITH CLAUS BARBIE!)

PANDA CLAUS (MOST OF OUR TOYS COME FROM CHINA, TOO.)

CROONER CLAUS (THE SHMALTZY LOUNGE ACT IS ALWAYS A HOLIDAY FAVORITE.)

CANTOR CLAUS (A SINGING RABBI WOULD BE A NICE CHANGE.)

BUDDHA CLAUS (AT LEAST WE KNOW HE'S GOT GOOD KARMA.)

BUBBIE CLAUS AND ZAYDE CLAUS (HO HO OY!)

SANTA MONICA CLAUS (THIS DUDE DELIVERS HIS GIFTS ON A SURFBOARD.)

BARBRA CLAUS (FUNNY GIRL FOCKER OR YENTL CLAUS, STREISAND IS SAINTLY.)

SANTA CLAWS (THIS CAT WON'T SCRATCH YOU OFF HIS LIST.)

SANTA PAWS (DOG SPELLED BACKWARDS IS YOU KNOW WHO!)

HARRY MEETS SALLY CLAUS

HANUKKAH HARRY (A.K.A. "THE HANUKKAH MAN") is Santa Claus's lesser known Jewish counterpart. It's been said that Harry is eight times busier than Santa… and with less help. Hanukkah Harry dates back to the 1950s when baby boomer parents, hoping to quell "Santa envy" in their children, concocted the stories to compete with "gentile" holiday customs. Some Jewish parents went to great lengths, even arranging for chimney drops from "Uncle Harry, the Hanukkah man."

Hanukkah Harry made prime time on a *Saturday Night Live* skit. John Lovitz portrayed the elusive Harry as a thin man with a scraggly gray beard, wearing a vest and a blue-and-white flecked hat. Harry rides around in a flying wagon pulled by donkeys Moshe, Herschel and Shlomo, delivering toys to Jewish children around the world. Sadly, no one has yet brought Hanukkah Harry to the big screen, until now…

INTRODUCING WHEN HARRY MET SALLY CLAUS:

After a long struggle with Alzheimer's, Rabbi Harold's dear wife, Hanna, slipped away.

Harold, better known to millions of Jewish children as "Hanukkah Harry," sat shiva in his Antarctic outpost for a very long time.

One day, Harry was taking his afternoon walk when he came across a laptop PC partially buried in the sand. It wasn't a Mac, but that's life. He figured it must belong to one of the "seasonal" scientists at the base, but now the facility was locked up tight for the winter. Harry decided to keep the laptop safe until spring.

Back home, Harry, a traditionalist who had stubbornly resisted hi-tech gadgets, turned on the computer and found that he could pick up a WiFi signal. He listened and connected and surfed… remembering that during his most recent eight-day trip to America, many young people on his route requested membership to a Jewish matchmaking service called J-Date.com. Deciding enough time had passed since Hanna's passing, he logged onto J-Date, and signed up. It couldn't "hoit," right? Of course right!

On the opposite side of the world, Sally Claus was trying to put the pieces of her life back together again. She and her husband of many, many years had split. Scandal!

Sally had only recently begun suspecting something wasn't kosher with Mr. Claus.

For centuries, Santa had always returned home promptly after his annual round-the-world business trip. Over the past couple of decades, however, he frequently called at the last minute to say he'd been delayed and needed to work late, night after night after night. Sometimes right up until the day after Valentine's Day!

This year, while she was washing his red suit (he'd FedExed it back) Sally thought she detected the faint smell of perfume mixed in with the usual chimney creosote. Then she received a package marked "personal." There was no return address, but the stamp had been cancelled with a Beverly Hills postmark. Inside, she found a collection of *Playboy* magazines—all December back issues. Her heart pounded as she slowly browsed the pages tabbed with yellow Post-It notes. There were cartoons that depicted her husband in various compromising situations with skimpily clad young women.

Sally almost fainted when it hit her: South of the Arctic Circle, Santa had a reputation as a womanizer and philanderer. You think you know a person.

When Santa finally arrived home (even Rudolph looked somewhat spent), Sally confronted him: "I see where you've been sleeping! I know that you're a fake." She proffered the evidence.

He tried to dodge the bullet by bellowing "Ho Ho Ho Ho Ho!" but Sally was furious. "You better watch out," she scowled, and a week later, Santa was served with papers. "Oh, for goodness' sake," he pouted as he checked them twice. He knew all too well that Mrs. Claus had crossed him off her list.

For Sally, life with "the fat man" had started to go wrong long before her discovery of his infidelity. She recalled the first red flags during the early part of the twentieth century when Santa accepted work posing for department store catalogs. Over the years his modeling career hit the big time. He was ubiquitous, appearing on buses, billboards, animated films and television commercials. His nonstop public jollity belied an increasingly disconnected home life. Santa, supposedly a symbol of good will toward man, was becoming more and more the symbol of unabashed commerce. Sally was losing respect for her husband...

Sally asked, "What about me?"

As time went by, Kriss Kringle's ego seemed out of control. Like a narcissist rock star, he refused to cut his hair and beard. His trademark outfit, the fashionable and festive red suit Sally had designed for him when they were newlyweds, now seemed cheesy and clichéd. Increasingly, Santa preferred

the company of that shiny-nosed Rudolph, Rudolph's girlfriend, Vixen, and their caribou pals. He often stayed out late, smoking corn cob pipes with that frosted snowman from down the street. When the Clauses sat down for dinner, they had little to talk about beyond "the list." The passion had gone out of the marriage.

Sally made out well in the divorce. Despite everything, Santa remained a generous, giving man. Sally got the sleigh, half the reindeer herd, the workshop and, because of global warming, a large tract of seasonal ocean-front property.

Santa retained the intellectual property rights and trademarks for Kriss Kringle and Father Christmas. Despite the blow to his family image, his Christmas spokesman contract was renewed. With help from the elves, Santa relocated his massive distribution operation to a former underground nuclear testing facility in the Nevada desert, not far from Las Vegas, which was becoming all the rage again.

But Sally grew lonely and her responsibilities weighed heavily. The expansive property was too much for one woman. She missed having a man around the house. She yearned for someone who loved children and knew his way around a snow blower. She had read an article in Reader's Digest about how people were meeting over the Internet.

. . .

Sally found a new Web site called Chrismukkah.com. It described a holiday that was becoming popular with people who celebrated both Christmas and the lesser-known festival called Hanukkah. While Sally had never met a Jewish person, she was fascinated by stories about "Hanukkah

Harry," a man who, much like her ex-husband, ran a holiday express delivery service. She found a link to his e-mail and fired off a note. She attached her photo, a flattering one taken only a few centuries before.

"You've Got Mail!" The computer startled Harry from his afternoon nap. The message read, "To Handsome Hanukkah Harry. Season's greetings! If interested, please write back. XOXO. Sally@ northpole.com." There was a photo attached.

She didn't look Jewish. In fact, she didn't appear to be his type at all. When he had posted his ad on J-Date, Harry had fantasized about meeting a nice, eligible young woman, perhaps from the Falkland Islands or New Zealand. Somewhere within commuting distance. Oy, he hated the idea of a long-distance relationship, and this woman was not exactly geographically desirable. And, it must be said, while Harry was no Paul Newman, she was certainly no early-bird special.

A bigger concern was that Harry knew this woman's ex-husband—they were in the same biz. On occasion he had crossed paths with "Father Christmas" in the marketplace, exchanged a polite "Good Cheer"/"Shalom." He knew Claus had a reputation as a jolly, flamboyant folk hero. He was the big *macher* of the holiday express delivery business. Harry knew about the divorce from industry blog sites, and he didn't want to chance getting on Claus's bad side.

Harry was quiet, introspective, not particularly jolly; a guy who favored dark wool suits. While Santa loved publicity—even had a deal with NASA to map his progress each Christmas—Harry preferred to fly under the radar. Harry's modest niche

business had something like a 2 percent market share in North America, and much less elsewhere. "If I were a rich man..." he often mused.

But, after many musings, and countless "on the other hand" considerations, Mr. Hanukkah replied to Ms. Claus's e-mail.

That is how it began. They soon discovered they had much in common. They shared the same hopes and dreams. Even though, in so many ways, they were polar opposites, they sensed a magnetic attraction, an undeniable spark.

When Harry met Sally in the flesh, he was smitten. She was vivacious and yet demure. Though she had clearly lied about her age, it no longer mattered. He didn't think she looked a day over 300.

She liked his lean figure, his exotic Mediterranean looks and his sensitive eyes. He always seemed worried, carrying the weight of the world on his shoulders: "The ozone hole was big again today," he fretted, or, "Those emperor penguins are at it again... marching back and forth like that... attracting hordes of adventure tourists. Antarctica is going to the birds."

They decided to team up in business, too. Each year, the two of them set out on their cruise around the world, visiting the homes of millions of children and bringing light and cheer to every place they went. Theirs was a match made in heaven, and they lived happily ever after.

The End.

THE HANUKKAH MAN

We had just eaten dinner when the sound of jingling keys turning in the door lock signaled my father's arrival home from work. As usual, he was late, and I was in a state of manic impatience.

"Daddy, Daddy, Daddy!!!!"

I raced down the hall in my footsie pajamas, sliding across the waxed parquet floor and into his arms. When he kissed me, his cheek was scratchy and smelled faintly of Mennen Skin Bracer.

"Daddy, can we light the menorah now?"

It was the first night of Hanukkah, and since getting home from nursery school, I had been fixated on the eight blue-and-gold packages under the frosted white Hanukkah bush.

"Okay, in a minute," he said as he put me down and headed to his room to change. The phone rang and my mother answered it in the kitchen.

"Who is it? Yes, all right. I'll see if he's here... Ronnie, it's for you!"

She was smiling with a goofy look on her face, and I knew something was up. Nobody ever called for me. I didn't like talking on the phone. I held the receiver to my ear.

"Hello?"

A man's voice said, "Yah, is this Ronald?"

Having been repeatedly warned about talking to strangers, I was hesitant to answer, but the voice sounded so familiar. He spoke with the same funny accent my older relatives had. They were from a place called Germany.

Shyly, I replied, "Yes."

"I am the Hanukkah Man. Have you been a good boy?"

A born skeptic, I challenged, "Who is this, really?"

"Acch. I'm the Hanukkah Man!" he insisted.

Unconvinced, I said, "Okay."

"Be good to your mother and father and I will give you some nice presents for Hanukkah."

"Okay," I replied, taking no chances. I kept my cool, not wanting to appear silly, lest this be a hoax.

The Hanukkah Man asked to speak with my mother. She whispered a few words to the Hanukkah Man, then covered the phone and yelled to my father in the bedroom, "Fred, pick up the phone."

I said, "Mommy, who was that really?"

"It was the Hanukkah Man!" she said with exaggerated astonishment.

While I had a theory, I didn't know for sure. The Hanukkah Man never called me again.

A few months later, my brother Jeff was born.

Recently I called Jeff to ask about his recollections of Hanukkah. We hadn't ever talked about it as adults, and I wanted to compare notes. I hoped to clarify some vague details.

"Hey Jeff, do you have any idea who the Hanukkah Man really was?"

"Wah?" Jeff had no idea what I was talking about.

Apparently, the Hanukkah Man had never called him. Which surprised me. I didn't want to make my little brother jealous, so I quickly changed the subject.

But in a way, I was pleased.

Deck the Halls with Lots of Tchotchkes

"How touching to have the meaning of Christmas brought to us by cola, fast food, and beer.... Who'd have ever guessed that product consumption, popular entertainment, and spirituality would mix so harmoniously?"

—Calvin & Hobbes

Snazzing Up the Hybrid Home

Chrismukkah is the blend-o-matic holiday where bending the rules of tradition is the only tradition. Your standard Christmas has its traditions and Hanukkah's got its time-honored rituals, but Chrismukkah is totally customizable by you, the user.

Chrismukkah is the time of year to let your inner interior decorator out for a wild spree. Excess, mixed metaphors and cross-cultural confusion are the stylistic overstatements of the day. Light the lights. Fan the flames. The more tinsel the better! 'Tis the season where good taste takes a break. Even Charlie Tuna hangs out the "gone gefilte fishing" sign.

If you're the Martha Stewart type, head over to your neighborhood craft store and let your imagination go meshuggeh. If not, hit the big-box stores for the holidays, commercialized-style. You might also find some fun items at thrift shops—the more retro, the bettro. This is not a time to let holly-go-lightly. Load your shopping cart with glitter, paint, ribbon, balsa wood, candy canes of every shape and color, plastic mistletoe, gold mini trees, Styrofoam wreaths and more. Then shlep on over to your favorite Judaica store and pick up a case of menorah candles, a drum of dreidels and a sack of chocolate gelt. Say goodbye to your bland old holiday hand-me-downs and say howdy-ho to gaudy garlands, ostentatious ornaments, roaring wreaths and meretricious menorahs.

MATZO BREAD HOUSE

DIRECTIONS

Measure the bird house with the ruler, and cut a paper pattern to the exact size of each surface of the house.

Using the patterns as a guide, cut the matzo into shapes with the X-Acto™ knife and straight edge. Work carefully and slowly. Matzo crumbles and cracks very easily. Cut along the perforations where possible.

Check the fit of each cut piece of matzo to its corresponding surface. Then, using the hot-glue gun, apply matzo to the wood.

Hot-glue non-chocolate candy to the house. With the white glue, apply the rest of the candy. (Don't use hot glue on chocolate. What are you, stupid?)

Try to enjoy it even though it's a waste of good matzo.

MATERIALS

SMALL WOODEN BIRD HOUSE
(SOLD AT CRAFT STORES)

8 SHEETS OF 8.5 X 11" PAPER
(FOR PATTERNS)

SCISSORS

X-ACTO™ KNIFE WITH BLADES

HOT-GLUE GUN WITH GLUE STICKS

WHITE CRAFT GLUE (NON-TOXIC)

STRAIGHT EDGE RULER

BOX OF MATZO
(MANISCHEWITZ OR STREIT'S
UNSALTED RECOMMENDED)

CANDY, ASSORTED SIZES AND COLORS, SUCH
AS GUM DROPS, HANUKKAH GELT, CHOCO-
LATE NONPAREILS, CANDY CANES AND
PEPPERMINTS.

WARNING: *If you've never worked in low-rise construction, please be aware that matzo is much harder to cut than gingerbread. In the festive spirit of our litigious society, read all instructions and cautions on packaging. This project is not intended for children under the age of twenty-one. Small parts are a choking hazard. Do not leave glue gun unattended. Use safety goggles. Go home before it gets dark. Do not eat candy after you've brushed your teeth, or once it's been attached to the house. In the case of an emergency, seek immediate medical attention, preferably from a nice Jewish doctor.*

THIS YEAR

TROUBLE-SHOOTING

For irregular or curved surfaces, first dampen matzo in water until it is slightly soft and pliable. (Don't get it too wet or you'll have matzo brei.) Gently bend to shape and glue to surface. If the matzo cracks during construction, fill the crevices with a mix of wet matzo "mortar."

Oh! Tannenbaum, Oy! Rosenbaum
Bush, Shrub or Tree?

"To tree or not to tree" is just one of several December Dilemma conundrums experienced by mixed-religion families. Nothing captures the cozy essence of the season like a twinkling evergreen tree. Only the most hardened "bah-humbugger" could deny its timeless, festive appeal. From Turkey to Thailand, no matter the national religion, the Christmas tree, like Coca-Cola, has become ubiquitous.

As a kid, I had a "Weihnukkah Bush"—a six-foot plastic kumquat tree that my mother shlepped home from the store, where it had been reduced for final clearance. We did our best to disguise its citrus persona with hanging dreidels, peppermint sticks and mesh "Santa" stockings filled with Hanukkah gelt. My Jewish friends had never seen anything like it. My Irish and Italian friends had never seen anything like it either. My father's side of the family, more traditional Jews, just shook their heads in disbelief. But I loved our mish-mash family tree. Its origins were actually second generation: My mother grew up in Germany just as Hitler was coming to power. Her father was Lutheran, her mother was Jewish, and Mom had strong early memories of their half-Christmas, half-Hanukkah tree. By the time she turned seven, celebrating Hanukkah was no longer an option, and decorative trees were a luxury they couldn't afford.

While the "Hanukkah bush" has since become a common Jewish interpretation of the Christmas tree, many observant Jews think it's disrespectful and creates J-mas confusion for the children—just another sign of the decline of civilization.

I must admit getting a little squeamish the first time I came home to find a blinking, ornament-laden conifer plopped down in the middle of the living room. My wife was beaming. The tree made her so happy, there was no way I could object. Now, both the menorah and tree coexist gracefully in our home. I suspect any "Mukkah" living with a "Chris" knows what I'm saying. I would even venture to say that most Jews are used to the tidal wave of Christmas culture that sweeps over every-thing each December.

So then how did the Christmas tree, a universal icon of peace and harmony, recently become a centerpiece of the so-called War on Christmas? In his book *The War on Christmas*, John Gibson makes "the stunning and shocking revelation" that there is a "secular liberal plot to ban the sacred Christian holiday," warning that the ACLU and the Jewish Anti-Defamation League, among other "con-gregants," are conspiring to outlaw the Christmas tree and the "Merry Christmas" greeting. Gibson's flame is being fanned by a handful of xenophobic talk show pundits who are fueling the fear that Christmas is endangered.

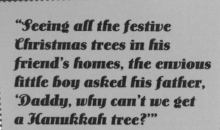

"Seeing all the festive Christmas trees in his friend's homes, the envious little boy asked his father, 'Daddy, why can't we get a Hanukkah tree?'"

"Startled, his father replies, 'Because the last time we had dealings with a lighted bush we spent forty years wandering around in the desert.'"

—OLD JEWISH JOKE

New
PATENT
PENDING
Hanukkah
TreeTopper™

This holiday reach for the star™

Which is where Chrismukkah comes in. Chrismukkah is the secular demilitarized zone; neutral, a Switzerland, if you will. Why waste all that time and money obsessing over the constitutional legality of Christmas trees in City Hall (and Hanukkah menorahs in the school hall) when there is an enlightened alternative? From Manger Square to Times Square, the all-inclusive, one-size-fits-all, multifaith Chrismukkah tree offers a peaceful solution. See, wasn't that easy?

When it comes to decorating the Chrismukkah tree, the solution is also easy. Menorahments! Part menorah, part ornament. To top it all off, we recommend a twin tree topper with double the stars, both a five-pointer and a Star of David. We're confident the whole merry mishpocha will approve.

Now, the only December Dilemma remaining is trying to figure out if it's better to go with that "faux fir" or "real" Chrismukkah tree.

"The Supreme Court has ruled that they cannot have a nativity scene in Washington, D.C. This wasn't for any religious reasons. They couldn't find three wise men and a virgin."

—JAY LENO

rner where you are

BAGEL MENORAHMENT

MATERIALS

BAGEL (DAY-OLD IS IDEAL)

CLEAR VARNISH OR POLYURETHANE

PAINT BRUSH

PLAID RIBBON OR YARN
    APPROXIMATELY 12" LONG

WHITE GLUE

SILK OR DRIED HOLLY, WITH BERRIES

DIRECTIONS

Brush bagel with varnish or polyurethane. Dry the bagel on a rack, then repeat the process.

When the bagel is dry, thread ribbon or yarn through the hole in the bagel. Make a loop and tie a bow at the top.

Glue a sprig of holly on the bagel and let it dry.

Hang on your Chrismukkah tree!

Tip: For an added touch of realism, take a bite from the bagel before you varnish it!

Chrismukkah goes green by hanging eco-ornaments made from recycled newspaper, bottles, cans and light bulbs. Edible lollypops and bagels too!

Menorah Pyro-Mania
Burn, Baby, Burn

"Come on baby, light my menorah." My 'tween mind envisioned the ghost of Jim Morrison prowling about our living room, wearing a yarmulke and tallis, flicking his silver cigarette lighter. It was the last night of Hanukkah, and for the past week, "The Doors," my first and best gift of the holiday, had been playing continuously on my portable record player.

According to Rabbi Cohen, I was about to become a man. On this last night of Hanukkah, in the last month of the last year of my boyhood, I was in a pensive mood as I watched the menorah flames flicker in the darkening living room. I was always fascinated by fire. Drips of red, yellow, blue and orange wax crept down the tilting candles, splattering onto the tinfoil spread below. I had an epiphany. The true miracle of Hanukkah was that more Jews didn't accidentally burn down their own houses.

After the last of the flames sputtered and died, I picked up Godzilla-with-radioactive-breath, my eighth and final gift, and went to my room.

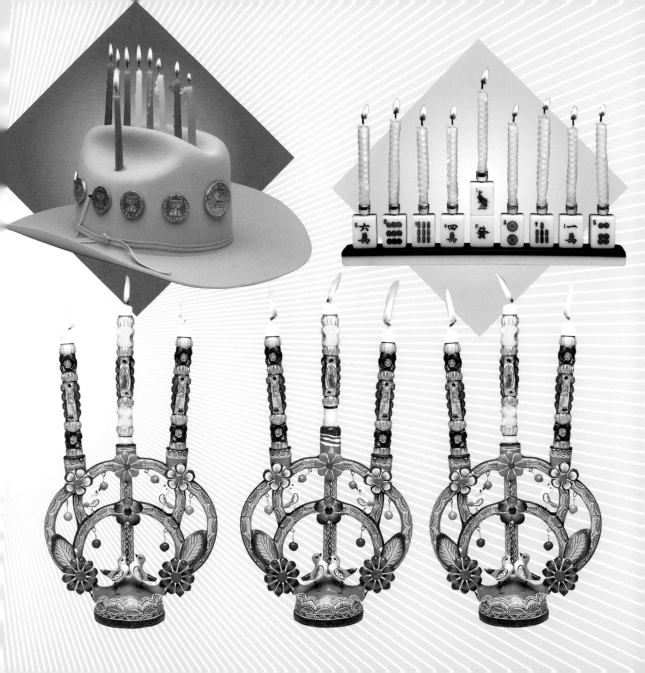

Many years have passed, but the candles still flicker and the music still plays. My three-year old daughter now holds the Shamash, recites the prayers, and cautiously lights each of the eight candles on her favorite menorah—the one shaped like a red New York City fire engine. I think she's inherited my childhood fascination with fire. The candlelight synchronizes with the twinkling electric bulbs of my wife's lavishly decorated Christmas tree, which stands on the other side of the living room.

The lighting of the Hanukkah menorah ("Chanuki-ah") is the central ritual in the observance of Ha-nukkah. Traditionally, on each of the eight nights of Hanukkah, all members of the family gather around the menorah at sundown. The Hanukkah

blessings are recited and then each person takes his turn lighting his personal menorah.

Chrismukkah combines the dual messages of Christmas and Hanukkah and wraps them in a one-size-fits-all, super-sized secular spree. Like the tree, the menorah is a key element. With Chris-mukkah, you can have your fruitcake and eat your latkes too, without guilt. Well, okay, maybe just a little guilt. After all, you could have invited your grandmother. Or at least called.

Kriss Kringle Kippahs
and Yarmulclaus Hats

If Chrismukkah is a celebration of diversity, then there's no better time to try a few different hats on for size. With so many millinery styles to choose from—beanies, bonnets, skimmers, bowlers, coonskin caps, fedoras, helmets and sombreros among them—standard-issue Santa caps or white nylon kippah caps just seem bland when they ought to be grand! Wimpy when it's time to be primpy!

Before we wave the magic wand and pull a rabbi out of a hat, here's a heads-up on holiday toppers:

The yarmulke (a.k.a., kippah, which is Hebrew for dome) is a slightly rounded skullcap worn by Jews when in temple. More observant Jews keep their kippah pinned to their heads from sun-up to suppah. While the yarmulke covers one's head to show respect for God, many like to show God their respect for the Yankees, Nike or the Rolling Stones by personalizing their yarmulkes. Branded logo yarmulkes are everywhere in Israel and orthodox communities in America.

While Web sites like LidsForYids.com cater to Jews, deacons and cardinals shop for their Zucchettos at CatholicSupply.com. Yarmulke-like Zucchetto skullcaps keep the shaved noggins of Catholic clerics warm in those unheated medieval churches and monasteries. They also denote rank by color: white for the Pope, violet for bishops, black for priests and red for cardinals… but you won't see many St. Louis Cardinals Zucchettos.

Hats off to Chrismukkah.

Dogma and Catechism

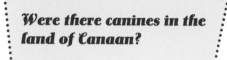

Were there canines in the land of Canaan?

Is your puppy taking Bark Mitzvah lessons? Does your cat attend Kitty Catechism? Have you been considering joining a pet-friendly congregation like All Saints Episcopal Church in Fort Lauderdale (Milk-Bones® and catnip provided at communion)? Before you do, just remember that while your dog may be faithful, you can't be as sure he has faith. This notion gives reason for paws.

Through the ages, dogs and cats have been both underdogs and top cats in the history of spirituality. In Chinese culture, feline figurines were used to ward off evil spirits, while to be born in the Year of the Dog means to possess the best traits of human nature. In ancient Egypt, the reigning cats and dogs were considered divine. There were doggie deities and a lynx sphinx. (In fact, not long ago, 300,000 feline mummies were unearthed in a cat catacomb near Cairo. Hello Kitty!)

In contrast, most biblical references to dogs are not so blessed. The Old Testament depicts dogs fiercely guarding the flocks of the tribes of Israel, but Hebrew tradition viewed canines as un-kosher, and never as companions. Given that both Joseph and Mary were Jewish, it's no wonder the nativity scene has cows, goats, camels and sheep witnessing the birth of Jesus, but dogs apparently were considered too mangy for the manger.

Now, it's time for all dogs, cats, hamsters and potbellied pigs to join the mixed-faith mish-mash revolution! Chrismukkah embraces all creatures, faithful and furry.

Here we share a few of our favorite photos from the Chrismukkah Barkmitzvakkah album.

Do beagles prefer bagels?

Can a cat from Katmandu convert to Catholicism?

LOX

happy holidays

happy holidays

happy holidays

happy holidays

Is that spitz a member of the tribe?

Can chickens be Wiccans?

bodhi

KOSHER

Can a gnu be a Jew?

SCHATZIE'S PSALM #23

The dog is my Shepherd,

I shall not flaunt,

He maketh me scoop poop
from green pastures,

He leadeth me to throw
sticks in quiet waters.

He drinketh from my toilet
bowl.

Gentile-Jew Hullabaloo!

A priest, a minister and a rabbi walk into a bar. The bartender looks at them and says, "What is this, a joke?"

Spinning the Dreidel
Under the Mistletoe

"For some it's about the baby in the cradle, while others much prefer to spin the dreidel."

—ANONYMOUS

Could it be that the dreidel—that ultimate Hanukkah symbol of fun and guilt-free gelt gambling—was actually the original Chrismukkah game? "Teetotum," a Christmas pastime involving a spinning top, was popular in Europe as far back as the sixteenth century. The word "dreidel" comes from the German *drehen*, meaning "to spin." Apparently the dreidel game is a German-Jewish variation of this Christmas tradition. Oy Tannenbaum, Hanukkah Harry!

Be it true or not, the Hanukkah dreidel has four sides, each symbolizing one of the ancient empires that enslaved the Jews: Babylonian, Persian, Greek and Roman. Like a spinning top, each eventually toppled and fell. The sides of the dreidel are printed with Hebrew letters: *nun*, *gimel*, *hay*, and *shin*. The letters form an acronym meaning "A Great Miracle Happened There." Where? Woflie's Kosher Deli in Boca? Don't be such a wise guy or I'll give you a klop to the head. Israel, of course!

Not surprisingly, some won't believe the German-Christmas origin of the dreidel. Their story goes like this: When the Syrian-Greek king Antiochus outlawed all Jewish customs, a group of young Jews resisted and continued to study the Torah. If a soldier approached, they would quickly clear the table and pull out the little spinning tops as though they were just playing a game. Those boy-chicks were nothing if not clever!

PHYSICS OF THE SPIN

Caution should always be exercised before attempting to spin the dreidel. This formidable game of chance relies on gyroscopic principles and one should thoroughly understand the underlying theory before engaging in spinning. We recommend you memorize this formula:

$$\tau = \frac{dL}{dt} = \frac{d(I\omega)}{dt} = I\alpha$$

ULTIMATE DREIDELS

- The world's largest spinning dreidel is 22' 2", built by Hillel in Montreal, Canada.

- Covered with more than 20,000 seashells and 13' high, the largest spinning crustacean-covered dreidel was made by Miami Beach artist Roger Abramson.

- Setting a record for the most simultaneously-spinning dreidels—541—is Temple Emanuel in Cherry Hill, New Jersey, on December 2005.

- For the fastest-spinning dreidel title, U.S. Astronaut Jeffrey Hoffman spun one in zero gravity on the space shuttle *Endeavor* in December 1993.

MAKE A DREIDEL OUT OF CLAY: CHRISMUKKAH EDITION

MATERIALS

ALUMINUM FOIL

SCULPEY CLAY (OR OTHER POLYFORM CLAY) IN ASSORTED COLORS

ROLLING PIN

PLASTIC KNIFE OR CLAY MODELING TOOLS

PENCIL

SCULPEY MATTE GLAZE, OPTIONAL

DIRECTIONS

Tear off a sheet of aluminum foil approximately 12″ long and crumple into a ball approximately 2″ in diameter. This will be the core of the dreidel.

Shape the foil core into a four-sided square cube with a pyramid on the bottom (like a dreidel).

Choose a base color for your dreidel. Blue is traditional, but lavender is also nice. Condition the clay by kneading it in your hands until it is soft and flexible.

Using the rolling pin, flatten the blue clay into a ¼″-thick sheet long enough to wrap around your foil dreidel, and high enough to extend top to bottom. Wrap it tightly around core and knead and smooth it into a clay dreidel. (You'll need to trim the excess.)

Make a spinner stem by rolling some clay into a 1½″ cylinder, about ¼″ in diameter. Poke your pencil into the top of the dreidel to make a hole for the stem. Insert about ½″ of the stem into the hole and smooth clay from top onto stem.

Now personalize your dreidel: Form pieces of colored clay into your choice of shapes to decorate each side of the dreidel. We suggest Hebrew letters, snowmen, Christmas trees, red stockings, menorahs or whatever spins your top.

Bake your dreidel according to package instructions on the clay.

When cool, brush on matte glaze (optional).

THE DREIDEL SONG
(CLASSIC VERSION)

I have a little dreidel,
I made it out of clay.
When it's dry and ready,
with dreidel I shall play.

Oh dreidel, dreidel, dreidel,
I made you out of clay.
Oh dreidel, dreidel, dreidel,
with dreidel I shall play!

It has a lovely body,
with leg so short and thin,
and when it gets all tired,
it drops and then I win.

Oh dreidel, dreidel, dreidel,
with leg so short and thin.
Oh dreidel, dreidel, dreidel,
it drops and then I win!

My dreidel's alway playful.
It loves to dance and spin.
A happy game of dreidel,
come play now let's begin.

Oh dreidel, dreidel, dreidel,
it loves to dance and spin.
Oh dreidel, dreidel, dreidel.
Come play now let's begin!

EXTENDED CHRISMUKKAH REMIX:

I have a second dreidel.
I made it out of pork.
It looked so appetizing,
I put it on my fork.

Oh dreidel, dreidel, dreidel,
I'm not supposed to eat,
Oh dreidel, dreidel, dreidel,
non-kosher kinds of meat.

My dreidel looked so yummy,
I put it in my mouth.
It tasted kind of funny,
I think it's headed south.

Oh, dreidel, dreidel, dreidel,
I'll give a little push,
Oh, dreidel, dreidel, dreidel.
You'll soon come out my tush.

NUN

GIMEL

HAY

HOW TO PLAY THE DREIDEL GAME

Any number of people may play, but the dreidel game is most efficiently played in groups of four to six. Traditionally, each player begins with an equal number of foil-wrapped chocolate coins, known as gelt. For Chrismukkah, gelt may be substituted with candy canes, gingerbread cookies, Hershey's kisses, popcorn, green, red, and blue M&Ms, or whatever your Bubbie sent you for the holiday season, including cubes of fruitcake or lavash.

1. Each player places a few gelt coins into a kitty.

2. Taking turns, each player spins the dreidel. When the dreidel stops spinning, whatever Hebrew letter is facing up determines the spinner's fate.

Nun means "nothing." Player wins nothing, loses nothing. Next player spins

Gimel means "whole." Players takes the entire kitty.

Hay means "half." Player takes half of what's in the kitty.

Shin means "put in." Player loses, and must put one coin into the kitty.

3. When only one piece of gelt is left in the kitty, each player adds another coin.

4. A winner is declared when one player has all the coins.

SHIN

Secular Harassment
in the Workplace

FROM: Sally Bishop, Director of Human Resources
SUBJECT: Company Christmas Party
DATE: November 30
TO: All employees

I'd like to express my gratitude to all for making me feel so welcome here at A.G.R. As one of my first duties, it's my pleasure to invite you to the annual AGR Christmas Party at Grace Bible Church (thank you Reverend Davies!) on December 20 at 2 PM. There will be a no-host bar and "special" eggnog at every table! Our own Laurie McVie will lead us through your favorite carols, and don't be surprised if Santa Claus himself drops by! It won't be a party without you!

FROM: Sally Bishop
SUBJECT: Happy Chanukah!
DATE: December 3
TO: All employees

I've received some comments about my last e-mail and I want to thank you for your candid feedback. I'd like to clarify that in no way did I intend to forget about or exclude any of our co-workers, so "Happy Chanukah" and "Shalem" to our Jewish associates. Be sure to introduce yourself at the Christmas party so we can *"smooze!"*

If I've missed anyone else's holiday, joyous *"whatever"* to you and yours!

FROM: Sally Bishop
SUBJECT: Christmas Party – New Name, New Location!
DATE: December 4
TO: All employees

In response to management's desire to celebrate the diversity here at AGR, I would like to announce that the Christmas Party will now officially be known as the "Holiday Event" and will be held at the Rotary Club instead of Grace Church! I've asked Laurie McVie to print up the lyrics to the "Dreidel Song" and "Kukumbuka Kwanzaa" so we can all join in after the caroling.

FROM: Sally Bishop
SUBJECT: Holiday Party Seating
DATE: December 6
TO: All employees

As requested by Doris in collections, I've reserved the table furthest from the dessert buffet for those enrolled in "Overeaters Anonymous." I've also received an anonymous note requesting a "sobriety table" for employees who are "twelve-stepping." I'm hoping you won't mind sharing with our pregnant employees. The alcohol-free table will be located next to the ladies' restroom, as requested by the employees who are "with child."

FROM: Sally Bishop
SUBJECT: Solstice
DATE: December 7
TO: All employees

Ms. Incantatrix from food service reminded me that December 21st is the Winter Solstice. To accommodate our pagan employees, I have arranged for a drumming circle following the singing. I did check, but the new nonsmoking laws prohibit the burning of sage incense inside the hall. However, a section of the parking lot will be set aside for any goddess associates who wish to partake in the burning of a Yule log.

BTW, the rumor that turkey has been eliminated from the menu because of a protest from vegan co-workers is false. It is true, however, that we've added an "animal-free product" buffet.

FROM: Sally Bishop
SUBJECT: Holiday Event
DATE: December 10
TO: All employees

Responding to concerns expressed by a few employees, we've removed the holiday tree, menorah, and manger scene from the lobby. Also, as you probably know, FOX News broke a sensational story about "Kriss Kringle's" dark side, revealing that Santa is an anagram for "Satan." In anticipation of the backlash, our legal-affairs department has recommended cancellation of CEO Richard Douglas' planned appearance as "the man in the red suit."

FROM: Sally Bishop
SUBJECT: Boycott Alert
DATE: December 12
TO: All employees

I've been asked to distribute a copy of the following press release:

(Tupelo, MS) - Parochials for Responsible Evangelism in Business and Society (P.U.R.E.B.S.) is calling for a boycott of all AGR products because the company has removed the word "Christmas" from its employee party. PUREBS is promoting the boycott to the 18.8 million PUREBS.org online supporters and on their nearly 400 radio stations nationwide.

I regret to announce that production will be shutting down until further notice. We are hoping to avoid long-term layoffs. I will update you as soon as I know more.

FROM: Richard Douglas, CEO
SUBJECT: Sally Bishop
DATE: December 13
TO: All employees

Earlier today, I accepted Sally Bishop's resignation. I know I speak for all of us in wishing Ms. Bishop best of luck in her future endeavors. Regretfully, in light of the layoffs, the board has decided to cancel this year's company holiday event. We sincerely hope this change will not offend anyone.

FROM: Richard Douglas
SUBJECT: Boycott ends
DATE: December 14
TO: All employees

I am pleased to announce that PUREBS has decided to end its boycott of AGR products.

In other news, I would like to announce that Donna Cassidy has joined AGR as our new Director of Human Resources.

FROM: Donna Cassidy, Director of Human Resources
SUBJECT: Christmas Party!
DATE: December 15
TO: All employees

I'd like to express my gratitude to all for making me feel so welcome here at AGR. As one of my first duties, it's my pleasure to invite you to the annual AGR Christmas Party at Grace Bible Church (thank you Reverend Davies!) on December 20 at 2 PM. There will be a no-host bar and "special" eggnog at every table! Our own Laurie McVie will lead us through your favorite carols, and don't be surprised if Santa Claus himself drops by! It won't be a party without you!

TOP TEN WAYS TO KNOW YOU'RE AT A LAME CHRISMUKKAH OFFICE PARTY:

10. You get there and it's just you, a bowl of chopped liver, and that IT guy dressed up as Santa.

9. The receptionist brings her famous mincemeat blintzes for the potluck.

8. There's mistletoe hung between two mezuzahs.

7. The company menorah is a bunch of coke bottles duct-taped to a Yule log.

6. The music stops until someone rehits the demo button on the "Dancing and Singing Santa."

5. Thousands of believers crash the party when someone notices one of the deep-fried latkes resembles a weeping Virgin Mary.

4. Your boss generously offers his cigar to light the menorah.

3. After mixing shots of Mogen David and Jagermeister, the entire accounting department is excused from the party for sexual misconduct while playing "Pin the Yarmulke on Rudolph."

2. You get a gefilte fruitcake from your Secret Santa.

1. There's not enough alcohol to last even one night.

YULE PLOTZ EGGNOG

SERVES 8 TO 12

Drinking too much of this potent drink during the winter solstice might indeed cause you to "plotz," or explode.

4 CUPS HALF-AND-HALF (OR MILK)

1½ CUPS SUGAR

12 LARGE EGG YOLKS

½ CUP DARK RUM

½ CUP BRANDY

¼ CUP BOURBON

2 CUPS HEAVY CREAM

1 PINT PREMIUM VANILLA ICE CREAM, MELTED

FRESHLY GRATED NUTMEG

In a large saucepan over medium heat, stir the half-and-half (or milk) with the sugar until the sugar dissolves and the mixture is hot. Remove pan from heat and set aside.

In a medium mixing bowl, whisk the egg yolks. Gradually whisk in a few tablespoons of the hot half-and-half/sugar mixture, helping to warm the eggs but not cook them. Whisk in the rest of the half-and-half mixture slowly, stirring constantly until combined.

Pour the mixture back into the saucepan and cook over low heat for 3 minutes, stirring constantly, until it reaches 180° F and is thick enough to coat the back of a spoon. Don't allow the mixture to boil.

Strain into a clean, medium bowl and allow the eggnog to cool completely. Whisk in the rum, brandy, and bourbon. Cover and refrigerate until well-chilled, at least 4 hours.

In a chilled, medium bowl, beat the heavy cream just until stiff. Fold into the chilled eggnog mixture. Pour into a punch bowl, add melted vanilla ice cream, and stir gently until incorporated. Grate the nutmeg over the eggnog, and serve.

Note: Eggnog should be consumed within 24 hours.

BIBLE BELT GELT MELT

SERVES 2

Here is a hybrid holiday hot chocolate with a kick. This nicely balanced drink will go over equally well in Cedarhurst, Long Island or Covington, Kentucky.

½ CUP HEAVY CREAM

1 CUP WHOLE MILK

4 CHOCOLATE GELT COINS

2 TABLESPOONS COCOA POWDER

2 TABLESPOONS KENTUCKY BOURBON

4 TEASPOONS GALLIANO

2 TABLESPOONS RUM DARK

Whip half the cream in a bowl until it is thick enough to hold its shape.

Unwrap the chocolate gelt and heat it and the milk in a saucepan over low heat, stirring, until the chocolate has melted.

Whisk in the cocoa and bring to a boil.

Remove from heat and stir in the bourbon, rum, Galliano and remaining cream.

Pour into two warmed mugs or glasses and top each with a generous spoonful of whipped cream.

"In the old days, it was not called the Holiday Season; the Christians called it 'Christmas' and went to church; the Jews called it 'Hanukkah' and went to synagogue; the atheists went to parties and drank. People passing each other on the street would say, 'Merry Christmas!' or 'Happy Hanukkah!' or (to the atheists) 'Look out for the wall!'"

—DAVE BARRY

MERRYSCHEWITZ MULLED WINE

SERVES 8 TO 12

Traditionalists might consider our muddled mulled wine recipe the "Nightmare Before Chrismukkah," but actually, it's not half bad.

1 ORANGE

1 LEMON

¾ CUP WATER

½ CUP SUGAR

4 CINNAMON STICKS

⅛ TEASPOON ALLSPICE

5 WHOLE CLOVES

1 BOTTLE MANISCHEWITZ™ CONCORD GRAPE

1 BOTTLE CHRISTIAN BROTHERS™ CABERNET SAUVIGNON

Zest the peels of the orange and lemon, avoiding the bitter white pith.

Cut remaining fruit into slices and set aside.

In a large saucepan, bring the zests, water, sugar, cinnamon, allspice, and cloves to a slow boil for 5 minutes. Remove from heat.

Add wine and fruit to the spice mixture, and simmer on low heat for 40 minutes. Do not allow the wine to boil.

Strain into a punch bowl and serve.

HAVA TEQUILA SUNRISE, SUNSET

SERVES 1

"Sunrise, Sunset" is one of the best-known songs from the vintage musical *Fiddler on the Roof*. Set in a small Jewish village in Russia in 1905, the play is about a family living and celebrating life, even while under Tsarist rule. "To life!" mirrors the meaning of Hanukkah.

2 TABLESPOONS GOLD TEQUILA

2 TABLESPOONS LEMON JUICE

4 TABLESPOONS ORANGE JUICE (FRESHLY SQUEEZED)

2 TABLESPOONS HONEY

2 TABLESPOONS GRENADINE

ICE CUBES

Pour the tequila, lemon and orange juice into a tall glass.

Add a few ice cubes and stir.

Trickle honey into the center of the drink. It should sink and create a layer at the bottom of the glass.

Quickly add the grenadine in one pour, sliding it down the back of a spoon into the bottom of the glass.

Done correctly, the grenadine will create a glowing layer above the honey at the bottom of the glass before rising.

PASSION OF THE ICED

SERVES 2 TO 4

Jesus Cohen! This spin on a Long Island Ice Tea will make your head spin like a dreidel.

2 TABLESPOONS VODKA

2 TABLESPOONS TEQUILA

2 TABLESPOONS RUM

2 TABLESPOONS GIN

2 TABLESPOONS TRIPLE SEC

3 TABLESPOONS SWEET AND SOUR MIX

2 CUPS PASSION FRUIT JUICE

ICE CUBES

Mix ingredients into a shaker over ice. Give one brisk shake.

Pour into a glass.

Garnish with lemon.

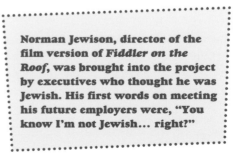

Norman Jewison, director of the film version of *Fiddler on the Roof*, was brought into the project by executives who thought he was Jewish. His first words on meeting his future employers were, "You know I'm not Jewish... right?"

GWYNETH PALTROWITCH

SERVES 2

This drink is named in honor of the beautiful and talented half-Jewish American princess Gwyneth Paltrow, daughter of Brooklyn-born director Bruce Paltrow and Tony award-winning actress Blythe Danner.

1 CINNAMON STICK

1 CUP WATER

¼ CUP FINE SUGAR

4 PINK GRAPEFRUITS (OR 2 CUPS GRAPEFRUIT JUICE)

1½ CUPS FRESH OR FROZEN RASPBERRIES
(OR ½ CUP RASPBERRY JUICE)

2 TABLESPOONS RUSSIAN VODKA

CRUSHED ICE

Put the cinnamon stick in a small pan with the water and the sugar. Heat gently until the sugar has dissolved, then bring to a boil for 1 minute. Remove cinnamon stick and allow sugar syrup to cool.

If using fruit, cut the grapefruits in half and juice them. Crush the raspberries in a blender or food processor and strain, or use a juicer. If using juice, skip this step.

Pour juices into a small pitcher.

Add syrup and vodka to the pitcher of juice.

Serve the drinks over crushed ice.

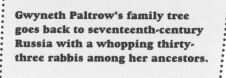

Gwyneth Paltrow's family tree goes back to seventeenth-century Russia with a whopping thirty-three rabbis among her ancestors.

SEAN PENN

SERVES 1

Oscar-winning Jew-tholic (Jewish-Catholic) actor/
director/activist Sean Penn no longer drinks, but
his rebelliousness is the stuff of legend.

He'brew Beer comes in three flavors, all certified
kosher and microbrewed at the Anderson Valley
Brewing Company in Boonville, California. Genesis
Ale is a nicely balanced amber ale. Messiah Bold,
a brown ale, is the beer you've been waiting for.

1 SHOT OF PADDY™ IRISH WHISKY

CHASE WITH PINT OF HEBREW™ GENESIS ALE

1 SHOT OF STOLICHNAYA™ RUSSIAN VODKA

CHASE WITH PINT OF HEBREW™ MESSIAH BOLD

REPEAT AS REQUIRED.

> **Penn's grandparents once ran a Jewish deli in
> New York, easily qualifying him for the honor
> of his own Chrismukkah drink. In recent
> years, Penn has been an outspoken critic of
> American foreign policies. His *refusenik* roots
> run deep: His father was Leo Penn, a Jewish
> film director of Russian descent who was
> blacklisted during the McCarthy era.**

IRVING BERLIN

SERVES 2

A Chrismukkah happy hour would not be complete without something from the famously Jewish creator of that bestselling Christmas song of all time, "White Christmas."

2 SMALL ORANGES

⅔ CUP LIGHT CREAM

FRESHLY GRATED NUTMEG

½ TEASPOON GROUND CINNAMON

½ TEASPOON CORNSTARCH, DISSOLVED IN TABLESPOON OF THE CREAM

2 EGGS, SEPARATED

2 TABLESPOONS BROWN SUGAR

2 TABLESPOONS BRANDY

Zest and juice the oranges.

Combine cream, nutmeg, cinnamon and cornstarch in a small saucepan and add the zest. Heat slowly on low, stirring frequently until bubbling.

In a medium bowl, combine egg yolks with brown sugar and whisk. Set egg whites aside.

Stir a few tablespoons of the hot citrus cream mixture into the egg yolks. Add the rest slowly, stirring constantly.

Return the mixture to the saucepan. Add the orange juice and brandy, and heat over low heat, stirring frequently until slightly thickened. Strain into a bowl and return to low heat.

Whisk the egg whites in a large, clean bowl until foamy and light.

Whisk a few tablespoons of the cream mixture into the egg whites to combine. Whisk the rest in carefully, stirring constantly to avoid cooking the egg whites.

Stir gently and pour into handled glasses or mugs. Sprinkle nutmeg on top before serving.

Berlin was born in Russia in 1888, and his family emigrated to New York when he was five. As a young child, Irving spent Christmas days with his neighbors, the O'Haras. He was captivated by their Christmas tree, which towered over him. Berlin later married Ellen Mackay, who came from a wealthy Catholic family. Their mixed marriage was a scandal at the time, and Mackay's father disinherited her.

SHIRLEY TEMPLE EMANUEL

SERVES 1

Here's a nice Chrismukkah drink for the children, or anyone else who feels like they'd rather sit at the kids' table.

1 CUP SELTZER, GINGERALE OR 7-UP
2 TABLESPOONS GRENADINE SYRUP
1 SLICE ORANGE
1 RED MARASCHINO CHERRY

Mix soda and grenadine.

Serve in tall glass with straw, garnished with orange and cherry.

> *Growing up in New York City in the era before Starbucks, the choice was much simpler. "Cawfee reg-u-la" meant a cup of caffeine with milk and two sugars, and "decaf" meant a cup of hot water with an orange packet of Sanka.*

MESHUGGEH NOG LATTE

SERVES 2

Whenever we'd go out for a big family birthday meal at Luchows, or some other fancy-shmantzy downtown restaurant, after the main course all the grownups would order Sanka and light up their cigars and cigarettes. My grandfather would have said this coffee eggnog concoction was "meshuggeh."

2 TEASPOONS SANKA™ DECAFFEINATED INSTANT COFFEE
2 CUPS MILK
2 CUPS PREPARED EGGNOG
CHOCOLATE SYRUP
FRESHLY GRATED NUTMEG

Measure 1 teaspoon Sanka™ into each of two large mugs.

Heat the milk in a small saucepan or in microwave. Cover to keep warm.

Warm the eggnog in a separate saucepan or in microwave. Do not allow it to boil.

Carefully pour the warm eggnog into a blender, and blend until very frothy.

Pour 1 cup of hot milk into each cup.

Top off with the frothy eggnog.

Garnish with a spiral of chocolate syrup and nutmeg and serve immediately.

Oy to the World!

Long before Adam Sandler coined "The Chanukah Song" or Kyle Broflofski of *South Park* crooned "A Lonely Jew on Christmas," Jews had a long, proud, and somewhat dysfunctional tradition of writing and performing some of the best Christmas songs and albums ever, including these gems:

IRVING BERLIN: "WHITE CHRISTMAS"

SAMMY CAHN: "LET IT SNOW"

SAMMY DAVIS JR.: "HERE'S A KISS FOR CHRISTMAS"

NEIL DIAMOND: *THE CHRISTMAS ALBUM*

JOAN JAVITS: "SANTA BABY"

BARRY MANILOW: "BECAUSE IT'S CHRISTMAS"

JOEY (HYMAN) & THE RAMONES: "MERRY CHRISTMAS (I DON'T WANT TO FIGHT TONIGHT)"

AL STILLMAN: "THERE'S NO PLACE LIKE HOME FOR THE HOLIDAYS"

ALLAN SHERMAN: "THE TWELVE GIFTS OF CHRISTMAS"

BARBRA STREISAND: *A CHRISTMAS ALBUM*

PAUL SIMON AND ART GARFUNKEL: "STAR CAROL"

HERB ALPERT & THE TIJUANA BRASS: *CHRISTMAS ALBUM*

MEL TORME: "CHESTNUTS ROASTING ON AN OPEN FIRE"

MARC (FELD) BOLAN & T. REX: "CHRISTMAS TIME"

Continuing the tradition, with a little shmaltzy twist, here are my favorite Chrismukkah songs, each destined to become a new holiday standard.

DECK THE HALLS

Deck the halls with lots of tchotchkes,
Fa la la la la la la la oy.
'Tis the season to eat latkes,
Fa la la la la la la la oy!

Shop the malls at risk and peril,
Fa la la la la la la la oy.
Make up words to Christmas carols,
Fa la la la la la la la oy!

IT'S THE MOST MESHUGGENAH TIME OF THE YEAR

It's the most meshuggenah time of the year.
Many gifts I'll be buying
And latkes need frying
'Cause Chrismukkah's here.
It's the most meshuggenah time of the year.
To the mall I'll be shlepping,

You know I'll be kvetching.
The roads will be jammed driving home,
Then back out I'll be going,
Menorah's not glowing · · ·
I'm all out of candles you know.
OY.
It's the most meshuggenah time of the year.
My children are bumming
'Cause Santa's not coming
With all his reindeer.
It's the most meshuggenah time of the year.

THE CHRISMUKKAH SONG

Latkes frying on the open fire,
Reindeer prancing in the snow.
My wife, Carol, sings in her church's choir
While my menorah candles glow.
And so we juxtapose · · ·
A dreidel with some mistletoe
Helps to make the season right.
I might plotz hanging wreaths and red bows.
The kids are fast asleep tonight,
While on a red-eye flight,
They know that Bubbie's on her way
With those outmoded toys they won't want to play
And their grandmother's gonna cry
When no one wants to taste her homemade matzo brei.
And so I'm kvetching through the holidays
With kids half-Christian and half-Jew.
Our in-laws say, "Peace on Earth"
And, "Oy Vey!"
Merry Chrismukkah to you.

'Twas the Night Before Chrismukkah ✡

MIDNIGHT MASS CONFUSION

On Christmas Eve, the trees are lit, fireplaces are warmed, friends and families are gathered, carols are sung, midnight mass is enjoyed, and cookies and milk are left for Santa.

Meanwhile, Jews go out for Chinese and a movie.

So what does one do on the night before Chrismukkah? Good question. Since Chrismukkah begins on the first night of Hanukkah and no one ever does anything on the night *before* the first night of Hanukkah, this becomes something of a conundrum... pa rum pum pum pum.

To be on the safe side, we recommend leaving a nice glass of soymilk and fortune cookies for whomever or whatever drops down the chimney.

THE NIGHT BEFORE CHRISMUKKAH

'Twas the night before Chrismukkah, and
    me, being Jewish,
I was "on call" again, and feeling quite
    blueish,
My wife had flown home to hang stockings
    with kin,
Secure in the knowledge St. Nick would
    pop in.

I lit my menorah, the candles burned down,
But then there was nothing to do in this town.
The malls and the theaters were all closed
    up tight;
There wasn't a bar that was open that night.

Some music could raise me, some hip-hop
    or swing,
So I searched through the paper, but there
    wasn't a thing.
Outside the front doorstep sat three feet of
    snow;
With the windchill included, it was twenty
    below.

Well, all I could do was sit there and brood,
When into my head popped a voice—Chinese
    food!
So I ran to the closet for hat, scarf and boots,
The better to cover my head, neck and suit.

I zippered my coat, all puffy with down,
And headed down Broadway to the old side of
    town.
The night it was freezing, so I caught the next
    train,
But all I could think of was Chicken Lo Mein.

I got off in Chinatown and rushed through the
    maze,
Past bakeries, markets, stores and cafes.
And they were all open: Which one? Can't de
    cide!
I chose Hunan Garden, and ventured inside.

The people were friendly, their plates
    piled high,
With the best Asian food, this side of Shanghai.
There were spare ribs and scallops (sweet,
    sour and spice),
Wontons and tofu, chow fun and fried rice,
Kung Pao and Moo Shu and Shrimp Happy
    Delight,
But the Double-Cooked Pork just didn't
    seem right.

When I had decided, the waiter did call,
I said, "What the hell!" and I ordered them all.
And when in a while, the food was all made,
It arrived at my table in a nonstop parade.

I chopped with my sticks 'til my fingers
    got sore,
With half of my meal falling down on
    the floor.
So I swallowed my pride, feeling somewhat
    a dork,
And asked if my waiter could bring me a fork.

I ate 'til I burst and drank down my green tea,
So I barely had room for a fortune cookie.
But my fortune was truthful; even though it
    was rude,
As I read, "Pork is kosher, when it's in
    Chinese food."

With a mix of Tsingtao and MSG in my head,
I slipped and I slid and glibly I said,
As I carried my doggy bag home through
    the white,
"Shalom to you all—and to all a Good Night!"

Chrismukkah After Dark

It's just past midnight. The gifts are all wrapped, the menorah's dewaxed, and the ornaments are well hung from the tree. Now what? If you're not yet twenty-one, it's past your bedtime. Go to sleep.

But if you're of legal age, the night is young. Invite some friends over. Change into something a little more comfortable, dim the lights and put a log on the fire. It's time to put the X back in Chrismukkah! Whip out that dreidel and have some fun.

ICE BREAKER DREIDEL SHOTZ

Play a few rounds of dreidel using shots of Schnapps instead of gelt.

DREIDEL SUPER LOTTO

Turn the game high stakes, casino style, with a cold-cash kitty.

SANTA'S VICE SQUAD

You better watch out.
You better not flee.
You better not hide by copping a plea.

Santa Claus is going downtown.

He's making a list.
He asked Heidi Fleiss.
He's gonna find out
You got busted for vice.

Santa Claus is going downtown.

He knows with whom you're sleeping.
He sees you're on the make.
He knows that you're no badass hood
But just a shyster fake.

So, you better watch out.
You better be wary.
There's no alibi from Hanukkah Harry.

Santa Claus is going downtown.

SPIN THE DREIDEL UNDER THE MISTLETOE

The dreidel game gets to first base in this modified make-out remake of the classic party game "spin the bottle" and "seven minutes in heaven." Best played while sitting underneath mistletoe. Rules below:

Eight (or more, or less) players sit in a circle. Each one chooses to be one of four dreidel letters: Nun (nothing), Gimel (whole), Hay (half), Shin (put in).

The first player spins the dreidel. The letter facing up determines the person who will be the kissee. If two people have the same letter, the spinner chooses one.

The dreidel is spun a second time to determine the action.

Nun: No action. Turn goes to right of spinner.

Gimel: Seven seconds smooching in sin. The kissee then becomes the next spinner.

Hay: A three-second smooch. The kissee becomes the next spinner.

Shin: The kissee chooses which of the other players will be kissed by the spinner.

Game over when everyone is consumed by feelings of guilt, jealousy, embarrassment or lip numbness.

STRIP DREIDEL

Naughty! Keep an eye out on the chimney for unexpected drop-in guests. Rules below:

The players take turns spinning the dreidel. The letter facing up determines the spinner's fate.

Nun: Player takes nothing off. Next player spins.

Gimel: Player must remove two articles of clothing.

Hay: Player must remove one article of clothing.

Shin: Player gets to put one article of clothing back on.

The last player wearing any clothing is the winner.

MORDECHAI OF HOLLYWOOD— CHRISMUKKAH UNMENTIONABLES

There's an old joke about a Jewish merchant who gets stuck with a shipment of 20,000 bras, so he cuts them in half and sells them as 40,000 yarmulkes... with chin straps.

In a titillating twist on life imitating farce, www.Yarmulkebra.com now sells bras made from yarmulkes. Apparently a song by MC Paul Barman, a Jewish rapper from Jersey, inspired this Jew-cy bit of lingerie. (Available in sizes from AA Bat-mitzvah to DD Boobooshka.)

Naughty or nice... Do I have to decide right now?

Noel Nosh

Merryshewitz.
Chrismukkah Farms
Fruitcake

"So go ahead and eat already. Just don't forget to say grace."

—Half-Jewish Mother

GEFILTE GOOSE

SERVES 8

Gefilte fish was traditionally boiled and mashed fish, stuffed ("gefilte" is Yiddish for "filled") into a hollowed-out fish carcass. Today, however, this step is usually omitted, and instead, lumps covered with a slimy looking cold gelatin appear on your plate. Our hybrid recipe replaces fish with goose, as in "Christmas Goose."

1 GOOSE BREAST

1 ONION, PEELED AND CHOPPED

2 EGGS

2 TEASPOONS KOSHER SALT

½ TEASPOON FRESHLY GROUND BLACK PEPPER

2 TEASPOONS SUGAR

1 PINCH NUTMEG

1 TABLESPOON VEGETABLE OIL

½ CUP MATZO MEAL

4 CUPS CHICKEN STOCK, FOR POACHING

1 TABLESPOON FRESH PARSLEY OR GREEN ONIONS, CHOPPED

1 CUP PREPARED HORSERADISH SAUCE

1 CARROT, PEELED AND CUT INTO TRIANGULAR SHAPES

Coarsely chop the goose breast and place in the bowl of a food processor. Pulse until the goose is minced but not pureed. Remove the meat and set it aside in a medium-sized bowl.

Put the onion, eggs, salt and pepper, sugar, nutmeg, oil and matzo meal in the bowl of the food processor and process until smooth.

Using a spatula, fold the egg mixture into the minced goose until well mixed. Chill the mixture for 30 minutes.

Meanwhile, bring the chicken stock to a simmer in a large, deep saucepan.

Shape the dumplings by scooping the chilled goose mixture onto a warm spoon (dip in hot water to warm) and smoothing the top.

Using your finger, gently slide the mixture off the serving spoon and into the simmering chicken stock. Repeat in batches until all of the mixture is used.

Gently poach until the goose mixture is cooked through, about 20 minutes.

Remove each gefilte goose ball and serve warm, garnishing the gefilte goose with carrot triangles, green onion or parsley, and horseradish sauce.

WHAT AM I, CHOPPED LIVER?

SERVES 8

We give our chopped liver some new respect by spreading it onto a nice fresh butter croissant.

1 POUND CHICKEN LIVERS

2 TABLESPOONS OLIVE OIL

2 ONIONS, CHOPPED

1 CLOVE GARLIC, MINCED

1 TEASPOON KOSHER SALT

1 TEASPOON FRESHLY GROUND PEPPER

3 EGGS, HARD-BOILED, COOLED AND PEELED

FRESH PARSLEY, CHOPPED

CROISSANTS

Heat the oil in a large skillet and add the chicken livers. Sauté until cooked through and add the onions. Cook for 10 minutes over low heat and add garlic, salt and pepper.

Remove from heat and cool slightly.

Place the chicken liver mixture in the bowl of a food processor and process until pureed, stopping to scrape sides of bowl often.

Add the hard-boiled eggs and pulse until just chopped and mixed.

Taste and adjust the seasonings. Scrape into a bowl and chill until serving time.

Sprinkle with fresh parsley and serve on croissants.

A brief summary of every Jewish holiday:

They tried to kill us.
We won.
Let's eat.

CHEESE GELT

SERVES 12

Not to be confused with Jewish guilt, Hanukkah gelt is the foil-wrapped chocolate coins, or "loot" that children wager when playing the dreidel game. It symbolizes the booty awarded to the Maccabee soldiers. Chocolate gelt is to Hanukkah what Hillshire Farm™ cheese balls are to Christmas. Merge the two and you get cheese gelt.

1 CUP BUTTER

2 CUPS FLOUR

1 CUP CHEDDAR CHEESE, GRATED

½ TEASPOON GARLIC POWDER

1 TEASPOON ROSEMARY

1 PINCH CAYENNE PEPPER

Place all ingredients in the bowl of a food processor and pulse until dough forms into a ball.

Shape the dough into a log about an inch in diameter and wrap it tightly in plastic wrap. Chill at least 2 hours or overnight.

Preheat oven to 350° F. While it warms, line a baking sheet with parchment paper.

Slice the log into ¼" "coins" and place them on the baking sheet, ½" apart.

Bake until golden brown, 15 to 18 minutes.

Cool and store in an airtight container.

BUBBIE'S GANOUSH
SERVES 4

Baba ganoush is a dip, a spread or a flavorful side dish. "Bubbie" is the Yiddish word for grand-mother, and "Babas Ganoush" is slang for a pro-fessional wrestler who deliberately loses matches. I had to deliberately wrestle this secret recipe away from my grandmother, hence the name!

1 EGGPLANT

1 HEAD OF GARLIC

1 TEASPOON OLIVE OIL

2 TABLESPOONS TAHINI

THE JUICE OF 1 LEMON

1 TABLESPOON OLIVE OIL

½ RED BELL PEPPER, CHOPPED

SALT AND PEPPER

1 TABLESPOON FRESH PARSLEY, CHOPPED

¼ CUP FETA CHEESE, CRUMBLED

BAGEL CRISPS (OPTIONAL), RECIPE FOLLOWS

Preheat the oven to 350° F. While it is warming, line a baking sheet with parchment paper.

Prick the eggplant all over with a fork, and place it on the baking sheet.

Slice the top off the garlic, brush with olive oil, and wrap in foil. Place the garlic bulb on the baking sheet with the eggplant.

Roast the vegetables in the oven for 1 hour, or un-til eggplant is very soft. Meanwhile, if you're mak-ing them, prepare the bagel crisps (see recipe).

Remove the vegetables and cool.

Squeeze the garlic pulp into a large bowl and mash.

Cut the eggplant in half and press lightly with pa-per towel to remove excess moisture. Scoop the eggplant flesh into the bowl with the garlic and mash to desired consistency.

Add the tahini, lemon, olive oil, red bell pepper and stir well. Season to taste with the salt and pepper. Stir in the parsley.

Sprinkle top with crumbled feta and serve cold or at room temperature with bagel crisps or crackers.

BAGEL CRISPS

4 FRESH PLAIN BAGELS

2 TABLESPOONS OLIVE OIL

¼ CUP PARMESAN CHEESE, GRATED

Carefully slice bagels horizontally into 4 or 5 crisps.

Place on baking sheet, brush lightly with olive oil and sprinkle with cheese.

Bake in a 350˚ F oven for 12 to 15 minutes until golden brown.

Cool slightly and serve with spread.

DECK THE HALLS WITH BOUGHS OF CHALLAH

SERVES 8

Traditional Jewish meals begin with the breaking of challah, a sweet, golden egg bread. We've decorated our festive Chrismukkah challah with symbolic red and green icing and found that it makes a nice edible menorah.

2 PACKETS ACTIVE DRY YEAST (**4½** TEASPOONS)

1⅔ CUPS WARM WATER

⅓ CUP SUGAR

¼ CUP HONEY

½ CUP VEGETABLE OIL

3 EGGS, LARGE

2 TEASPOONS SALT

7 CUPS BREAD FLOUR, OR UNBLEACHED ALL-PURPOSE FLOUR

½ CUP RAISINS (OPTIONAL)

1 EGG YOLK, BEATEN WITH **1** TEASPOON OF WATER (FOR GLAZE)

1 CUP POWDERED SUGAR

WATER

RED AND GREEN FOOD COLORING

COLORED SPRINKLES

Combine yeast, ⅔ cup of warm water, and 1 teaspoon of the sugar in a large bowl, swirl to combine, and let rest for 5 to 10 minutes.

While yeast mixture is resting, line a baking sheet with parchment paper. Set aside.

To the yeast mixture, add the remaining water, sugar, honey, oil, eggs, salt, and 4 cups of flour. Beat the dough by hand or in an electric mixer with dough hook for 3 to 4 minutes until smooth.

Slowly add the remaining flour and beat with dough hook for 5 minutes or knead by hand for 8 to 10 minutes until dough is smooth and elastic. The dough should be slightly sticky, so resist adding more flour. Knead in raisins if using.

Shape the dough into braids: Divide the dough in half and set one half aside. Roll dough into a rectangle 15 inches long. Cut dough into three portions lengthwise. Press the top pieces together and begin braiding. Tuck each end under. Repeat with remaining half.

Place loaves on the baking sheet, cover with a clean towel, and let rise until doubled in size, usually 1 to 1½ hours.

Preheat oven to 350˚ F. Brush the loaves with the egg glaze and place in oven for 25 to 30 minutes until the loaves sound hollow when tapped. Cool on a rack.

In a small bowl, mix the powdered sugar with enough water to make a thin glaze. Divide it into two bowls, and tint one bowlfull red and one green, with the food coloring. Drizzle the glaze over the top and decorate with colored sprinkles.

MATZO BALL SNOWMAN

SERVES 4 TO 6

This is my family's secret matzo ball recipe, handed down from grandmother to grandmother. Made with real matzo, they are slightly spicy and much more flavorful than your average ball. Don't forget to start early—you've got to soak the matzo for at least a few hours or overnight.

4 MATZOS

WATER

2 TABLESPOONS CHICKEN FAT, BUTTER, MARGARINE OR OIL

1 ONION, FINELY CHOPPED

2 EGGS

SALT

GINGER

NUTMEG

CHOPPED PARSLEY

1 CUP MATZO MEAL

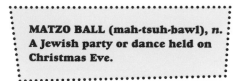

MATZO BALL (mah-tsuh-bawl), *n.* A Jewish party or dance held on Christmas Eve.

Place matzos in a shallow dish filled with room-temperature water. Leave overnight or until thoroughly soaked—at least a few hours.

Melt the fat in a large pan and add the onion. Cook until it begins to get brown and soft.

Meanwhile, squeeze all the water out of the matzos (use your clean hands) and add it to the pan with fried onions, stirring constantly, until moisture has evaporated and the matzo no longer sticks.

Place onion-matzo mixture in a large bowl. Stir in eggs, spices and parsley, and just enough matzo meal to hold it together. Refrigerate for at least one hour.

Bring water to a boil in a large pot. Add a dash of salt.

Meanwhile, remove the matzo ball mixture from the refrigerator. Reach into bowl and, with a tablespoon, scoop out a large walnut-sized ball of the mixture. Roll the dough between your palms to shape it into a ball. If it falls apart, add matzo meal until the mixture holds together. Place the ball on a cookie sheet or counter.

Repeat until you've used up all the dough.

Drop balls into the gently boiling water. Watch closely for the balls to rise to the top, about 20 minutes. Do not cover the pot!

When the balls rise, they are done cooking. Remove them with a slotted spoon and serve in broth as a soup, or use toothpicks to create whimsical Chrismukkah snowmen.

FA LA LA LATKES

SERVES 6

Our Fa La La Latkes, made from naturally nutritious sweet potatoes, may be served as a diplomatic alternative to Aunt Dorothy's marshmallow-studded casserole.

2 SWEET POTATOES, PEELED AND GRATED

1 SMALL YELLOW ONION, PEELED AND GRATED

2 GREEN ONIONS, CHOPPED FINELY

2 TABLESPOONS FRESH PARSLEY, CHOPPED

1 EGG, BEATEN

2 TABLESPOONS ALL-PURPOSE FLOUR

1 TEASPOON SALT

½ TEASPOON PEPPER

2 CUPS VEGETABLE OIL FOR FRYING LATKES

CRANBERRY APPLE COMPOTE (RECIPE FOLLOWS)

SUGAR PLUM FAIRY SAUCE (RECIPE FOLLOWS)

Place the grated sweet potatoes, yellow and green onions, and parsley in a large bowl and toss with the beaten egg.

Sprinkle the flour over the potatoes and toss well. Season with salt and pepper.

Heat the oil in a large, heavy cast iron or nonstick frying pan until very hot.

Using a measuring cup or large spoon, scoop about ½ cup of the potato mixture from the bowl and slide it into the hot oil. Repeat until pan is full, leaving about ½" between pancakes.

Cook until browned, 3 to 5 minutes. Flip, then cook the other side until golden and crisp. Remove from pan and place on plain brown grocery bags to drain.

Serve immediately with cranberry apple compote or sugar plum fairy sauce. Leftovers can be frozen for up to 1 month. Reheat in a 350° F. oven for 10 to 12 minutes until crisp.

CRANBERRY APPLE COMPOTE

2 CUPS CRANBERRIES

2 APPLES, PEELED AND CHOPPED

1 CUP SUGAR

1 TEASPOON CINNAMON

¼ CUP ORANGE LIQUEUR

Heat cranberries, apples, sugar and cinnamon in a saucepan on medium, stirring often, until berries have popped and sauce is thickened, about 8 to 10 minutes. Remove from the heat.

Stir in the orange liqueur.

Serve warm or cold with latkes. Can be made 3 days ahead and refrigerated in a sealed container until needed.

> Potato latkes, or pancakes, are to Hanukkah what turkey is to Thanksgiving. They are usually served with apple sauce (but never maple syrup), and can induce a case of heartburn for eight days and eight nights.

SUGAR PLUM FAIRY SAUCE

1 (12-OUNCE) PACKAGE FRESH CRANBERRIES

1 (16-OUNCE) CAN PLUMS, CHOPPED, WITH JUICE RESERVED

¼ CUP APPLE JUICE

1 CUP SUGAR

2 TABLESPOONS CRYSTALLIZED GINGER

1 PINCH SALT

Bring all ingredients to a boil in a saucepan. Reduce heat and simmer until berries have popped and sauce is thickened, 5 to 8 minutes.

Mash with a wooden spoon to desired consistency.

Serve warm with latkes. Can be made 3 days ahead and refrigerated in a sealed container until needed.

MATZA PIZZA

SERVES 8

"Matza" pizza pays homage to the Italian princes who welcomed Jews fleeing the Spanish Inquisition. Jewish-Italian history dates back thousands of years. This dish brings together the best of two cuisines—matzo balls and pizza. Mangi-oy!

1 PACKAGE DRY ACTIVE YEAST

1⅓ CUPS WARM WATER

2 TEASPOONS SALT

1 TEASPOON SUGAR

⅓ CUP OLIVE OIL

4 CUPS ALL-PURPOSE FLOUR

1 (16-OUNCE) JAR MARINARA SAUCE

16 MATZO BALLS, PREPARED AND SLICED LIKE PEPPERONI (SEE RECIPE, PAGE 112)

4 CUPS MOZZARELLA CHEESE, GRATED

1 TEASPOON DRIED BASIL

1 TEASPOON DRIED OREGANO

> **Q. What kind of cheese do you use on matza pizza?**
>
> **A. Matzarello.**

Whisk yeast and water together in a large mixing bowl and let sit for 5 minutes until mixture foams.

To the yeast and water, add salt, sugar, oil and 3 cups of the flour. Mix well with a wooden spoon.

Add the remaining flour and mix with hands until a very stiff dough forms.

Turn the dough onto a floured surface and knead for 5 to 6 minutes until smooth and elastic.

Wash out mixing bowl, and grease well with olive oil.

Place the dough in the greased bowl, cover with plastic and let rise for 1 hour in a warm place.

Preheat the oven to 400° F. Line a large baking sheet with parchment paper and dust with flour.

Punch down dough and remove it from the bowl. Stretch and push the dough into a 12" circle and brush with olive oil.

Pour the marinara sauce over the crust and arrange matzo ball slices on top.

Sprinkle the cheese over the top and scatter the herbs over the cheese.

Bake the pizza for 20 to 25 minutes until crust is brown and cheese is melted and bubbling.

Remove and cool for 10 minutes before serving.

BLITZEN'S BLINTZES
SERVES 8

Not to be confused with "blitzkrieg," the blintz is the Jewish answer to the French "crepe suzette," a thin pancake wrapped around a filling. The blintz trails the latke as a favorite holiday food, as Blitzen always follows Rudolph.

1 CUP FLOUR

2 EGGS

½ TEASPOON SALT

1 CUP MILK

2 TABLESPOONS BUTTER, MELTED

2 CUPS RICOTTA CHEESE

1 EGG YOLK

1 TEASPOON LEMON JUICE

1 TABLESPOON SUGAR

1 PINCH SALT

VEGETABLE OIL FOR FRYING

POWDERED SUGAR, FOR SPRINKLING

SOUR CREAM, FOR GARNISH

MANNY-CRANNY SAUCE (RECIPE FOLLOWS)

> When Joseph Stalin discovered that his food was being poisoned, he executed all six of his chefs and appointed a Russian Jewish boy as a replacement. The teen cooked only latkes and blintzes, and Stalin came to love them.

Whisk flour, eggs, salt, milk and melted butter in a mixing bowl until smooth. Refrigerate for at least 1 hour or overnight.

Meanwhile, prepare the filling: In a large bowl, mix ricotta, egg yolk, lemon juice, sugar and salt until smooth. Refrigerate until ready to use.

Heat 6″ omelet pan over medium heat and add a teaspoon of vegetable oil. Tilt to coat pan.

When pan is hot, pour in a thin layer of batter just to cover the bottom of pan and swirl gently to spread. Batter will set quickly and will brown slightly on the bottom.

Loosen the pancake with a spatula, and slide the pancake out of the pan onto a sheet of waxed paper. Repeat with remaining batter, layering with waxed paper.

Pancakes can be stored in the refrigerator overnight, frozen for two weeks (tightly wrapped) or filled right away.

TO FILL PANCAKES:

Lay one pancake on a flat surface and place 1 tablespoon of filling across the middle. Tuck in each side and roll up tightly.

Heat the oil in a large frying pan and add blintzes in a single layer without crowding. Cook for 3 to 4 minutes per side until golden brown.

Serve hot with sour cream, powdered sugar, and Manny-Cranny Sauce.

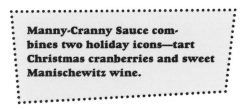

Manny-Cranny Sauce combines two holiday icons—tart Christmas cranberries and sweet Manischewitz wine.

MANNY-CRANNY SAUCE

SERVES 8

1 ORANGE

1 (12-OUNCE) PACKAGE FRESH CRANBERRIES

2 APPLES, PEELED, CORED AND CHOPPED

2 CUPS SUGAR

½ CUP MANISCHEWITZ CONCORD GRAPE WINE

Zest and juice orange.

Place all ingredients in a medium sauce pan and bring to a boil over medium heat. Reduce heat to low and stir often until berries pop and sauce thickens, about 8 to 10 minutes.

Remove from heat and cool for 10 minutes before serving. Can be made two days ahead and refrigerated.

GENERAL SAUL'S CHICKEN
SERVES 4

To Jews everywhere, Christmas Eve means just one thing: Chinese food! This spicy dish was invented in New York's Chinatown during the 1970s. The chef had an ironic sense of humor, for General Tso Tsung-tang was famous for his frequent bouts of dysentery.

1½ CUPS CHICKEN BROTH

6 TABLESPOONS SOY SAUCE

¼ CUP RICE WINE VINEGAR

¼ CUP SHERRY OR WHITE WINE

1 TEASPOON MINCED FRESH GINGER
    (OR ½ TEASPOON GROUND GINGER)

2 GARLIC CLOVES, MINCED

½ CUP SUGAR

⅔ CUP CORNSTARCH

1 EGG, BEATEN

2 LBS BONELESS, SKINLESS CHICKEN, CUT INTO 1 INCH
    CUBES (DARK MEAT IS TRADITIONAL)

1 CUP SCALLIONS OR GREEN ONIONS, SLICED

4 SMALL DRIED HOT CHILI PEPPERS

¼ CUP SESAME OR VEGETABLE OIL FOR DEEP FRYING

STEAMED RICE

Combine chicken broth, ¼ cup soy sauce, rice vinegar, wine, ginger, garlic, sugar and ⅓ cup cornstarch into a 1-quart jar. Cover and shake until mixed well. Set aside.

In a medium bowl, mix together the egg, 2 tablespoons soy sauce and ⅓ cup cornstarch.

Add chicken cubes and stir until coated evenly.

Heat oil in a wok (or large skillet) over high heat. Add chicken, with its egg marinade.

Stir-fry until each chunk is a crispy light brown and cooked through, about 5 to 8 minutes. Remove chicken and drain on paper towel.

Add chili peppers and green onions to the wok and stir-fry for 30 seconds

Add the chicken broth mixture to wok, stirring constantly until it boils. Sauce will thicken.

Place chicken back into wok and cook in sauce 1 to 2 minutes until hot and bubbly.

Serve over steamed rice.

> **"The problem with Jewish food is that two days later, you're hungry again."**
>
> **—OLD CHINESE PROVERB**

5767 (Year according to Jewish calendar)

– 4703 (Year according to Chinese calendar)

1064
(Total number of years that Jews went without Chinese food)

KOSHER FRUIT CAKE

My wife's "nutty as a fruitcake" recipe puts a kosher spin to a Christmas classic. To make the cake correctly, make sure all ingredients are kosher.

⅓ CUP DRIED APRICOTS

⅓ CUP CHOPPED DRIED CHERRIES

⅓ CUP DRIED CRANBERRIES

⅓ CUP DRIED APPLES

⅓ CUP RAISINS

1 CUP LIGHT RUM

2 CUPS ALL-PURPOSE FLOUR

½ TEASPOON BAKING POWDER

½ TEASPOON KOSHER SALT

½ TEASPOON GROUND CINNAMON

8 TABLESPOONS UNSALTED MARGARINE

¾ CUP PACKED BROWN SUGAR

8 EGGS

2 TABLESPOONS SWEET KOSHER WINE

¼ CUP UNSULFURED MOLASSES

⅔ CUP CHOCOLATE CHIPS OR CRUMBLED CHOCOLATE HANUKKAH GELT COINS

Soak the dried fruit in ½ cup of rum for at least a day, covered tightly at room temperature.

When you're ready to cook, preheat the oven to 325° F.

Grease a 9" round pan or a 8" x 4" loaf pan and line with parchment paper.

In a medium bowl, whisk together the flour, baking powder, salt and cinnamon.

In a large bowl, cream the margarine and sugar until fluffy, and slowly whip in the eggs.

Add the flour to the margarine mixture in three batches, alternating with the wine and molasses.

Stir in the dried fruit/rum mixture and chocolate chips or gelt.

Pour into prepared pan and bake for 55 minutes to 1 hour.

Let cake cool in the pan for 10 minutes, then sprinkle with 2 tablespoons of rum.

Place a piece of parchment paper large enough to wrap the entire cake on a flat surface. Lay a piece of cheesecloth the same size on the paper and sprinkle with 1 tablespoon rum.

Unmold the cake on top of the cheesecloth, and sprinkle top and sides of the cake with the remaining rum.

Wrap the cake, pressing the cheesecloth closely to the surface of the cake.

Place the cake in an airtight tin or plastic container and let it age for at least 4 weeks at room temperature. If storing longer, douse with additional rum for every 4 weeks of storage.

Johnny Carson joked every Christmas about the one fruitcake in the world that is passed from family to family.

JOLLY JELLY DOUGHNUTS

SERVES 10

Tasting much like a Krispy Kreme, "Sufganiyot" was introduced to Israel in the 1930s by immigrants from Germany, where jelly doughnuts are a New Year's tradition.

1 PACKAGE DRY ACTIVE YEAST

¼ CUP WATER, LUKEWARM

¼ CUP SUGAR

¾ CUP MILK

6 TABLESPOONS BUTTER, SOFTENED

2 EGGS

1 TEASPOON SALT

3¾ CUPS FLOUR

OIL FOR FRYING

1 CUP FRUIT JELLY, PLUM OR STRAWBERRY PRESERVES

GRANULATED SUGAR, FOR DUSTING

In a large bowl, mix together the yeast, water and 1 teaspoon sugar. Let sit for 5 minutes.

Add the milk, remaining sugar, butter, eggs, salt and 2 cups of flour and beat with wooden spoon until smooth.

Add the remaining flour and knead into a soft dough on a floured surface. Cover dough with a clean towel and let rise for about 1 hour in a warm place.

After it has doubled in size, punch down the dough and knead into a smooth ball. Roll it on a floured surface into a large circle about ¼" thick.

Cut dough into 3" rounds using a clean glass or cookie cutter, and transfer the doughnuts to a clean, floured surface.

Cover and let rise again for 30 minutes.

Heat 3" of oil in a skillet to 375° F.

Add the doughnuts in a single layer and fry until golden on both sides, turning once. Remove with a spatula to brown paper bags to drain.

Using a sharp knife, cut a slit into the side of each doughnut. Fill a pastry bag with the jelly and pipe into the center of each doughnut.

Sprinkle with sugar and serve warm.

CHALLAH STICKY BUN WREATH

SERVES 8

There's nothing like sticky buns on Christmas morning—and made with challah, they are destined to become a Chrismukkah tradition.

1 RECIPE CHALLAH DOUGH, RISING IN BOWL (SEE PAGE 110)

1¼ CUPS BROWN SUGAR

½ CUP HONEY

1 CUP BUTTER, MELTED

⅓ CUP SPICED RUM

2 CUPS PECAN HALVES, DIVIDED

¼ CUP GRANULATED SUGAR

1 TABLESPOON CINNAMON

While the challah dough is rising, grease two Bundt pans or one 9" x 13" pan with cooking spray or butter.

In a small bowl, mix ¼ cup brown sugar, honey, butter, rum and 1 cup pecans. Distribute in the bottom of the pan(s).

Pulse the remaining sugars, pecans and cinnamon in the bowl of a food processor until mixture is crumbly. Set aside.

After the dough has risen, punch it down and roll it on a floured surface into a large rectangle about ⅓" thick.

Sprinkle the crumbly sugar mixture over the dough, lightly pressing it into the dough and leaving 2" of dough along one long side.

Tightly roll the dough up jelly-roll style. Press the edges into the roll to seal.

Using a sharp, serrated knife, cut the rolls into 1"–thick slices and place over the topping, leaving room between each for rising.

Cover the rolls and let rise for 30 minutes.

Meanwhile, preheat the oven to 350° F.

Bake the rolls for 25 to 30 minutes until golden brown and remove from oven.

Cool 10 minutes and invert onto a decorative serving platter.

Serve warm!

Chrismukkah Listmania

"Sure I got a gift on Christmas, but for Hanukkah, I only got gifts on four nights."

—Jeff Kent, Half-Jewish comedian

Holy Half-Hebrew Hollywood!

*"Paul Newman's half-Jewish,
Goldie Hawn is too,
Put them both together,
What a fine lookin' Jew!"*

—ADAM SANDLER'S "THE CHANUKAH SONG"

When Adam Sandler's "The Chanukah Song" first started getting airplay in 1996, it was cause for Jewbilation. Sandler's song solidified the existence of the "Semi-Semite" within pop-culture. Jewish-Gentile intermingling is certainly nothing new, going all the way back to our "Main Mensch" Moses who married Zipporah, the daughter of a Midianite priest. Today, intermarriage accounts for nearly half of the knots tied under the Chuppah, and the half-Jewish offspring of mish-mash matrimony are a unique and rapidly growing demographic. Our fantasy holiday party guest list is a Who's Who of celebrity half-Jews likely to light both the menorah *and* the Christmas tree during Chrismukkah.

PAULA ABDUL
DON ADAMS
DAVID ARQUETTE
ROSANNA ARQUETTE
DAVID BLAINE
YASMINE BLEETH
ORLANDO BLOOM
LISA BONET
HELENA BONHAM CARTER
MATTHEW BRODERICK
NEVE CAMPBELL
PHOEBE CATES
    (BORN KATZ)
JOAN COLLINS
JENNIFER CONNELLY
HARRY CONNICK JR.
JAMIE LEE CURTIS

SAMMY DAVIS JR.
DANIEL DAY-LEWIS
ROBERT DE NIRO
MICHAEL DOUGLAS
DAVID DUCHOVNY
JON FAVREAU
CARRIE FISHER
HARRISON FORD
ADAM GOLDBERG
CHRISTOPHER GUEST
JAKE GYLLENHAAL
MAGGIE GYLLENHAAL
BECK
    (HANSEN)
GOLDIE HAWN
BARBARA HERSHEY
    (BORN HERZSTEIN)
XAVIERA HOLLANDER
KATE HUDSON
AMY IRVING
FRIDA KAHLO
BEN KINGSLEY
    (BORN KRISHNA BANJI)
KEVIN KLINE
LENNY KRAVITZ
MICHAEL LANDON
    (BORN EUGENE OROWITZ)
TRACI LORDS
BILL MAHER
BARRY MANILOW
JULIANNA MARGULIES
PAUL NEWMAN
SOPHIE OKONEDO
JERRY ORBACH

SHARON OSBOURNE
GWYNETH PALTROW
SARA JESSICA PARKER
SEAN PENN
ELVIS ARON PRESLEY
FREDDIE PRINZE SR.
RAIN PRYOR
ROBBIE ROBERTSON
GERALDO RIVERA
WINONA RYDER
    (BORN HOROWITZ)
J. D. SALINGER
ALICIA SILVERSTONE
CARLY SIMON
BEN STILLER
MATT STONE
OLIVER STONE
LINDSEY VUOLO
NOAH WYLIE

"Being half-Jewish,
I only have half the
hang-ups, but some-
times I feel twice as
guilty for only having
half the guilt."

–XAVIERA HOLLANDER

"CHRISMUKKAH COUPLE" QUIZIKKAH

Match the Hybrid Honeys to Their Show

1. DHARMA FINKLESTEIN AND GREG MONTGOMERY

2. KELLY CORCORAN AND LENNY CANTROW

3. VIRGINIA HILL AND BUGSY SIEGEL

4. JAMIE STEMPLE AND PAUL BUCHMAN

5. KIRSTEN NICHOL AND SANDY COHEN

6. WILL TRUMAN AND GRACE ADLER

7. IZZY GROSSMAN AND TYLER MOSS

8. CHARLOTTE YORK AND HARRY GOLDENBLATT

9. JULIE AND GABE KOTTER

10. ANDREA ZUCKERMAN AND JESSE VASQUEZ

11. PAM BYRNES AND GAYLORD "GREG" FOLKER

12. ANNIE HALL AND ALVY SINGER

13. CHERYL HINES AND LARRY DAVID

14. SALLY ALBRIGHT AND HARRY BURNS

A. ANNIE HALL

B. THE O.C.

C. CURB YOUR ENTHUSIASM

D. WHEN HARRY MET SALLY

E. DHARMA AND GREG

F. BUGSY

G. MAD ABOUT YOU

H. WELCOME BACK KOTTER

I. MEET THE PARENTS

J. WILL AND GRACE

K. SEX AND THE CITY

L. CROSSING DELANCEY

M. BEVERLY HILLS 90210

N. THE HEARTBREAK KID

ANSWERS

1. e; 2. n; 3. f; 4. g; 5. b; 6. j; 7. l; 8. k; 9. h; 10. m; 11. i; 12. a; 13. c; 14. d

THE CHRISMUKKAH GUIDE TO TALKING JEWISH (JEWBONICS)

"I'm not a real Jew. I just play one on TV." Such could be said for many an actor, including Irish-Catholic Peter Gallagher, who plays super-mensch Sandy Cohen on Fox's *The O.C.* He's got his Bronx-Yiddish vibe down, but for those of you who need more help, here are the inside secrets to talking Jewish.

1. Harden consonants at the ends of words.
EXAMPLE: "kosher restaurant" becomes "kosher restauranDT."

2. Pronounce the letter "W" with a "V" sound.
EXAMPLE: "wacko" becomes "vacko."

3. Pronounce "R" sounds with a guttural sound similar to gargling with mouthwash, represented in the example as "GGGH."
EXAMPLE: "Oh mine Godt!!!! Can't you see it's GGGHraining outside! Put on yourGGHrubbers!"

4. Pronounce "CH" like a cat trying to clear a furball from its throat.
EXAMPLE: "CHHrismukkah? Such CHHutzpah!"

5. Frequently begin sentences with the word "so" or "such."

EXAMPLE: "Such a big deal you've become!"

6. Answer questions with another question.
EXAMPLE: "How are you?" is answered by, "So, how should I be?"

7. Place the subject at the end of a sentence after a pronoun has been used in the beginning.
EXAMPLE: "She dances beautifully, that girl."

8. For emphasis, a word should always be repeated, replacing the first letter with a "shm."
EXAMPLES: "lawyer, shmawyer" or "Pulitzer, shmulitzer."

9. Pepper your sentences with Yiddish words (see Chrismukkah A to Z).

10. Whenever possible, be sarcastic or complain a little.

Some examples of standard English, followed by the Jewbonics equivalent.

"Sorry, I do not know the time" becomes, "What do I look like, a clock?"

"Goodbye and good luck" becomes "You should live to 120."

☆ Jack Frost in Translation

CHRISMUKKAH A TO Z

Every religion has its own language, so whether you're in a mixed marriage, cohabitating in hybrid sin (didn't you hear your bubbie/grammy's anguished sighs?), or hooking up with some hottie bombalottie who wouldn't know challah from holly, it's a good idea to learn some of your beloved's favorite phrases. Our hope is that this dual-purpose Sunday School and Yiddish 101 dictionary will help you part the treacherous waters of theological linguistics. Just remember these two golden rules:

1. A little bit of enlightenment goes a long way, but a little bit of Yiddish goes further.

2. Better to have a tongue in cheek than a foot in mouth.

GOLD=Sunday School.

PURPLE=Yiddish 101.

AMEN: The one part of a prayer that everyone knows. In Hebrew "Omain." Not to be confused with Lo Mein, a food traditionally eaten by Jews on Christmas Eve.

ANGEL: Benevolent celestial winged being that acts as a go-between, between heaven and earth.

ANTICHRIST: Parental euphemism for Barney, the purple dinosaur.

APOCALYPSO: A cosmic cataclysm in which Harry Belafonte destroys the ruling powers of evil.

BAPTISM: The Christian ritual symbolizing admission into the Church, traced back to the Jewish cleansing ritual of Mikvah.

BAT/BAR MITZVAH: *Bar* for boys. *Bat* for girls. Bark for dogs. Ceremony, usually at age thirteen, marking entry into adulthood.

BAGELA: Gay Jewish baker.

BLASPHEMY: The defamation of the name of God. Some states still have blasphemy laws on the books.

BOYCHICK: A Jewish expression of affection, equivalent to "buddy" or "kiddo."

BRIS-AND-TELL: The unsolicited, painfully-detailed description of a child's circumcision, generally told by the child's parents.

BRUCHAH: Blessed. Most Jewish prayers begin with it: "Baruch atah Adonoi" means "Blessed art thou, O Lord."

BUBBIE: An older woman who thinks your children are perfect even though she's sure you're not raising them right.

BUBKES: Nada, nothing, zilch. As in "You're gonna sue me?! You know what you'll get? *Bupkes!*"

CAROL: To sing in a loud, joyous manner. To go from house to house singing Christmas songs.

CHAZZEREI: Swill, pig slop, unpalatable, rotten. "No wonder my son is getting fat! All my daughter-in-law feeds him is *chazzerai!*"

CHEX MIX: A common Christmastime snack in the Midwest, made from a General Mills cereal.

CHRIST: Jesus' last name.

CHUPPAH: Wedding canopy, under which the bride and groom and rabbi stand during the ceremony.

CHURCH: The synagogue where gentiles go to worship.

CHUTZPAH: Brazenness, gall, nerve.

CLERGY: Professionals who are in the God business.

CONFESSION: Disclosing one's sins to a priest for forgiveness. A less expensive alternative to psychoanalysis.

CONFIRMATION: A Christian ceremony, usually performed at the age of twelve, admitting a person to full membership in a church. Very similar in meaning to a Jewish Bar/Bat Mitzvah, though uses much less glitter on the invitations and, for girls, less glitz in the dress.

DAMNATION: Go directly to Hell. Do not pass God.

DAVEN: To pray in the synagogue.

DIOCESE: An area of many parishes presided over by a bishop.

DIVINITY: Holiness, piousness, goody-goody-ness.

DRECK: Cheap, junky, lousy, worse than shlock. Also, insincere talk or excessive flattery.

DUMKOPF: Dumbbell, dunce, dumb head.

ECH: A groan, a disparaging exclamation of distaste.

EVANGELIST: One who assures us of salvation, while damning the neighbors.

EXCOMMUNICATION: When one is given the silent treatment by one's upset girlfriend or wife.

FA LA LA LA LA: Christian equivalent to the Jewish "Yiddle-diddle-diddle-diddle"

FAITH: The quality that enables one to explain the unknown by means of the unobservable. Where your eyeth, nothe and mouth are located.

FALSE PROPHET: A corporate accountant who cooks the books to give the appearance the company is doing better than it really is.

FANCY-SHMANCY: Pretentious, ostentatious, over the top. "So, another *fancy-shmancy* Chrismukkah party?"

FARMISHT: Confused, befuddled, dysfunctional.

FARKLEMPT: Overwrought, on the verge of tears, all choked up.

FARCOCKT: Messed up. "It used to be a great holiday, but now it's all *farcockt*."

FEH: An expression of distaste or disgust.

GENTILE: All people who are not Jews.

GEVALT: What happened? Can also be used with "Oy" for added effect.

GOSPEL: Good news. Referring to the belief that Christians have forgiveness of sins through Jesus.

GOY: From the Jewish perspective, a non-Jewish person. Plural is *goyim*.

GRACE: A short blessing said before or after a meal.

HALACHA: The complete set of Jewish laws.

HALLELUJAH!: An expression of joy, praise and thanks. Antonym for "Oy!"

HEAVEN: The cheesecake at Cantor's Deli on Fairfax in L.A.

HEBORT: To forget all the Hebrew one ever learned immediately after one's Bar Mitzvah.

HEDONISM: The teaching that pleasure is the principal good and proper goal of all actions.

HEEB: Formerly a slur to describe a Jewish person, it's come into vogue among younger Jews who use it to describe themselves and each other. Also a hipster magazine about Jewish culture.

HELL: The future place of eternal punishment of the damned including the devil and his fallen angels. Featured in a very funny comic strip by Matt Groening.

HERESY: Opinion or doctrine at variance with established religious beliefs, especially dissension from or denial of Roman Catholic dogma by a professed believer or baptized church member.

HEYMISH: Homey, friendly

HOLY WATER: A liquid with the chemical formula H_2OLY

HYMN: A song of praise, usually sung in a key three octaves higher than that of the congregation's range.

IBBLEDICK: Unwell, out of sorts, nauseated. The typical feeling a Jew has the first time he learns that Jesus died for his sins.

IMMACULATE CONCEPTION: The belief that Jesus was conceived without original sin (i.e., sex).

JESUS: Popular slang describing the act of doing something so effortlessly that it seems to be a miracle. Used most effectively when the jesuser has no idea how it worked so well. "How'd you get here so fast through that traffic? I *jesussed* myself here." Also, Christ's first name.

JEWBILATION: The thrill a Jew feels upon finding out a favorite celebrity is Jewish.

JEWDO: A traditional form of self-defense based on talking one's way out of a tight spot.

JEWFRO: An afro on a Jewish person. Very popular with Jewish ultimate frisbee players.

JEWLICIOUS: A very attractive person who is Jewish.

KIBBITZ: To chat, gab, engage in frivolous conversation. What WASPs like to do during cocktail hours before the holiday dinner. Not to be confused with *kibbutz*, a farm in Israel.

KNISH: Baked dumpling filled with potato or meat. More varieties of it than Dunkin has donuts.

KOSHER: Cool, with the flow, nice. Can also refer to food that has been blessed by a rabbi.

KVELL: To beam with pride and joy at someone, usually one's child. "My son came all the way from California to visit me for Chrismukkah! I'm *kvelling*!"

KVETCH: Whine, complain; whiner, a complainer. "My new daughter-in-law doesn't want to have a bris for the baby. I don't mean to *kvetch*, but can you imagine?"

L'CHAIM!: A popular toast that means "To life" in Hebrew.

LUMINARIES: The candles that line driveways and sidewalks during Christmas. For Chismukkah, use black-and-white cookies for candleholders..

MARTYR: Someone who sacrifices herself for a belief or cause. A stereotypical Jewish mother.

MAZEL TOV: Good luck, congratulations.

MATZILATION: Smashing a piece of matzo to bits while trying to butter it.

MEGILLAH: The whole, long, drawn out, complicated mess.

MENSCH: A caring, decent person—man or woman—who can be trusted.

MERCY: Act of not administering justice when that justice is punitive.

MESHUGGEH: Nutty, wacky, crazy. "Boy oh boy, she really has some *meshuggeh* ideas."

MEZUZAH: A little container put in the doorframe that blesses a Jewish house.

MIRACLE: An out-of-the-ordinary divine intervention in the world, such as beating a hand of four kings and an ace with four aces and a king.

MISCHEGAS: Madness, insanity, absurd, ridiculous, eccentric behavior. "What is this *mischegas*? Hanukkah and Christmas combined into one holiday?"

MISTLETOE: 1. A person with a severe foot injury. 2. A disease that afflicts astronauts.

MISHPOCHA: The extended family. "For the holidays, I invited the whole *mishpocha*."

MITZVAH: A good deed. Giving to charity is a *mitzvah*. Rubbing your partner's back is a *mitzvah*. A Jewish baptism.

MORALITY: An instinctive sense of right and wrong that tells some people how everyone else should behave.

MORTAL SIN: A serious transgression of God's Law that can damn someone to eternal hell.

NACHES: Joy, gratification, especially from children. "Only three years old and already he can read! He gives me such *naches*!"

NEBBISH: A nobody, weakling, awkward person, someone you pity, Woody Allen-esque.

NEW TESTAMENT: The Christian bible written sometime after the birth of Christ.

NOSH: To have a little snack between meals. A snack, a small portion.

NOEL COWARD: Someone who is afraid of Christmas.

NU? So? Well?

NUTCRACKER SUITE: Fancy hotel room where wealthy squirrels stay.

ORIGINAL SIN: The state humans are born into according to the New Testament.

OY: An exclamation to denote disgust, pain, astonishment or rapture.

PARADISE: Like where you are right now, only much, much better.

PEW: A medieval torture device still found in Catholic churches.

PLOTZ: To explode, burst from good news. "You got front row tickets for Streisand! I'm *plotzing*!"

PIETY: Reverence for the Supreme Being, based upon His supposed resemblance to Man.

PRAY: To ask that the laws of the universe be annulled on behalf of a single petitioner.

PRIEST: Cheesy heavy-metal band from the 1970s.

PROPHET: Doctrine of corporate ethics.

PSALM PILOT: A digital book of the Bible from which passages are often quoted.

PUTZ: A jerk, an idiot, a fool with no real power, except to make your life unpleasant.

RAPTURE: Person who is obsessed by hip-hop music.

REFORMED: A synagogue that closes for the Jewish holidays.

REBBE: A nebbishy rabbi.

REDEMPTION: To free someone from bondage. To get something at a discount by using coupons.

REPENT: To turn away from sin.

RESURRECTION: To be raised from the dead.

ROSARY: Catholic word referring to a string of beads that is used to count prayers as they are recited.

SACRAMENTALS: Special prayers, deeds, or objects used to gain spiritual benefits from God.

SALVATION: Christian term meaning redemption and deliverance from suffering, evil and death.

SHALOM: Peace (a watchword and a greeting).

SHANAH TOVAH: Hebrew greeting of "Happy New Year."

SHAYGETZ: Non-Jewish male

SHIKSA: A non-Jewish female.

SHLEP: To drag, carry or haul with great effort. To travel long distances.

SHLOCK: An inferior product, junk, cheap-o, as in "Next Chrismukkah, less *shlock* for the children, okay?"

SHLEMIEL: Clumsy bungler, an inept person, butter-fingered, dopey.

SHLIMAZEL: Person with perpetual bad luck (the shlemiel spills the soup on the shlimazel).

SHLUMP: Careless dresser, untidy person; as a verb, to idle or lounge around. "It's not a real holiday, but do you have to dress like such a *shlump*?"

SHMEAR: The business; the whole works; to bribe. The amount of cream cheese (but never mayo) the deli puts on your sandwich. "I'll have a bagel with a *shmear*."

SHMALTZY: Sentimental, corny. "Oy that movie *It's a Wonderful Life* is so *shmaltzy*!"

SHMINGLE: Shmooze + mingle. What people do at the office Chrismukkah party.

SHMUTZ: Dirt, filth. "I just put on this blouse, and already I'm covered in *shmutz*."

SHMUCK: Literally, the snipped skin from a bris. A vulgar word for a silly person.

SHPIEL: A long, involved story or tale. "Don't give me a whole *shpiel*."

SHTUP: Push, shove, slang for sex. "No chuppa, no *shtuppa*."

SHUL: Yiddish for synagogue. The church where Jews pray.

SIN: Anything that is contrary to the law or will of God.

SON OF GOD: The title for Jesus Christ.

SYN-AGOG: Jewish person who is astonished to find they have been immoral.

TALLIS: Rectangular prayer shawl with fringes on each of its four corners, worn during prayer.

TEMPTATION: That which moves someone to sin.

TEN COMMANDMENTS: The most famous top-ten list not seen on David Letterman.

TORAH: The first five books of the Old Testament hand-printed on a large scroll.

TRINITY: The belief that describes God as three persons in one: the Father, the Son, and the Holy Spirit.

TSORIS: Troubles, misery, problems, woes.

TUCCHIS: J-Lo, rump, kiester, bum, buns, cheeks, rump.

TUMEL: Confusion, noise, uproar.

TZEDAKAH: Spirit of philanthropy, charity, benevolence

VO DEN: What did you expect? So what else?

WRATH: On the sixth day, God created man. On the seventh day, he realized his mistake.

YAHWEH: Expression of joy shouted by Jewish rodeo cowboys. Also another name for God.

YARMULKE: A traditional Jewish skullcap, a.k.a. Yid Lid, Kippa, Yar.

YENTA: Gossipy woman, a blabbermouth.

YESHIVAH: Post-graduate Hebrew school.

YIDDISH: The traditional language of organized complaint. A tongue that never takes its tongue out of its cheek.

YIDDLE-DIDDLE-DIDDLE-DIDDLE: Jewish equivalent to the Christian "Fa La La La La La."

YIDENTIFY: Discovering someone's Jewish ethnicity even though their names are Curtis, Davis or Taylor.

YULE LOG: Forest service record book of the number of Christmas trees cut down each year.

ZAYDE: Man who performs lame tricks like finding a quarter in one's ear, or pretending to pull one's nose off. Any older relative adored by children during the holidays.

More Merry Mish-Mash Mayhem

SCHLOMO HANUKKAH — SANTA CLAUS — KWANZAA GUY

CAN'T WE ALL JUST GET ALONG?

So now we know how a typical American mish-mash family celebrates Christmas and Hanukkah together. But Jews have been wandering the world for thousands of years, and the world is a pretty big place. While the large majority of the estimated 14.6 million Jews worldwide have made their home in North America and Israel, more than 3 million others spin the dreidel in more exotic locales. Consequently, matrimonial mingling goes far beyond the shiksa-blonde/menschy-mama's-boy media stereotype we are so familiar with. From Jew-mai-can Rasta-matzah pairings to Singapore-Semites to Moldovian-Mogen Davids, the festive possibilities cannot be covered by Chrismukkah alone. Accordingly, here are a few new hybrid holidays we'd like to see.

KWANZAAKAH

Combining the seven nights of Kwanzaa with the eight nights of Hanukkah, this double-identity cultural holiday is celebrated by Hebrew hip-hop families and self-proclaimed "Jewlattos." Both Jews and African Americans historically experienced slavery followed by freedom and forced displacement from their homeland. Kwanzaa features the Kinara, a seven-branch candle holder that resembles a menorah, except with red, green and black candles.

BUDDHAKKAH

Celebrated by enlightened Bu-Jews, this "Zen-Judaism" holiday harmonizes Hanukkah with the December 8th holiday called Bodhi Day. About 300 years before Judah, Prince "Sid" Siddhartha spent eight days and nights thinking about his future under a nice bodhi tree. There he had an epiphany, and faster than you can say, "Zen-Amen!", he began teaching the "Four Noble Truths" that became the foundation of Buddhism:

1. Everyone suffers.

2. Suffering comes from ignorance.

3. It's not too late. Your ignorance can be overcome.

4. Follow the eight-fold path, and you won't be ignorant and suffer.

Is it me, or does this sound familiar?

Celebrating Buddhakkah traditionally includes an Ashtanga yoga class at the JCC, take-out Chinese (preferably Buddha's Delight), and enlightening the eight-fold path candles of the zen-menorah after sunset. The eldest celebrant present recites the blessing: "Do not kvetch. Be a kvetch. Become one with your kvetching!"

HINDUKKAH

India has historically been a refuge for people of many religions, creeds and beliefs. Hinduism, Jainism, Buddhism, Sikhism were born in India. Judaism, Islam and Christianity arrived from outside. Today, India is a truly integrated secular nation.

As in Hollywood, Jews played a major role in Bollywood. Until recently, it was taboo for Hindu women to act in films, and so most of the early superstars, including Firoza Begum, Ruby Meyers and Patience Cooper, were Jewish. Had they married Hindus, they'd be Hinjews.

WIKKAKKAH

Bewitching half-Jewish goddesses like Natalie Portman, Scarlett Johansson, Gwyneth Paltrow and Winona Ryder are not uncommon, but finding a nice Jewitch girl is not so easy. The spellbinding Willow Rosenberg on television's *Buffy the Vampire Slayer* comes to mind. Wicca, which traces its roots to pre-Christian, northern European pagan beliefs, may seem an odd mix with Judaism (Jewish Shabbat meets the Black Sabbath) but don't dismiss it. Wicca is said to be the fastest growing religion in America, and with growing concern about the stagnating Jewish population due to low birth rates, casting a fertility spell might not be such a bad idea. So let's all do a sacred circle dance around the burning menorah and boil a cauldron of nice chicken soup.

KABBALATOLOGY DAY

Kabbalah has become very trendy of late. Followers of the esoteric, mystical offshoot of Judaism include Madonna, Britney Spears and Demi Moore. Another celebrity-rich religion, scientology boasts eight million members including Tom Cruise, Lisa Marie Presley, John Travolta and Jenna Elfman. Critically acclaimed musician Beck was raised in a Jewish-Scientologist home, and we couldn't help but wonder what would happen if Kabbalah and Scientology merged. At the very least you'd have a heck of a holiday party invite list.

NON-RAMADANAKKAH

Ramadan is a month of prayer and fasting that takes place during the ninth month of the Islamic calendar. It commemorates when Allah revealed the Qur'an to the prophet Muhammad. Since Islam uses the lunar calendar, Ramadan moves each year and it very rarely overlaps with Hanukkah, thus Ramadanakkah isn't on our list. However, in the event Muslims and Jews ever make peace in the Middle East, we might reconsider.

AGNOSTAKKAH

Surrealistic film director Luis Buñuel once famously declared, "Thank God, I'm an atheist." While atheists are certain that God doesn't exist, agnostics are more iffy, believing that God's existence can neither be proven nor disproven. *I don't know & you don't either* is a popular Agnostic bumper sticker. The newest nonreligion is Universism, whose manifesto declares: "Universists deny the validity of shared revelation, faith and dogma." We're pretty sure they'd embrace Agnostakkah, an eight-day holiday celebrating nothing.

BAHÁ'Í MITZVAH

Bahá'í is an all-you-can-eat faith smorgasbord incorporating the teachings of all the biggies. Adam, Noah, Zarathustra, Krishna, Abraham, Moses, Buddha, Jesus, and Muhammad are all served. Bahá'í believes that each prophet brought fresh new revelations, messengers will continue to come into the unborn reaches of time, all people are equal, and the unity of humanity transcends race, nation, gender and class. Diversity, like flowers, adds color to the beauty of a garden. Who could argue with such idealism? Well, most of my relatives. They could argue about anything.

ChrismuhanukwanzaramadanaBahai'nukkah Day anyone?

Chrismukkah Help Line

RESOURCES

ajc.org - AMERICAN JEWISH COMMITTEE

amnesty.org - AMNESTY INTERNATIONAL
Working to protect human rights worldwide.

au.org - AMERICANS UNITED FOR SEPARATION OF CHURCH AND STATE

dovetailinstitute.org
DOVETAIL INSTITUTE
Serving the interfaith community.

halfjew.com - HALF JEW
A Web site about being half-Jewis

heebmagazine.com - HEEB MAGAZINE
Jewish culture humor magazine.

humanrightswatch.org
HUMAN RIGHTS WATCH
Defending human rights worldwide.

interfaithfamily.com - INTERFAITH FAMILY
Serving Jewish interfaith marriages.

jewhoo.com - JEWHOO
A Jewish alternative to Yahoo.

jewlicious.com - JEWLICIOUS
Just like the Jewish people, only bloggier.

jewsweek.com - JEWSWEEK
Popular Jewish blog site.

joi.org - The Jewish Outreach Institute.

mazeltovcocktail.com
MAZEL TOV COCKTAIL
Radical Jewish culture.

mixedrace.com - MIXED RACE
Web site for people of mixed cultural backgrounds.

mnsu.edu - RELIGIONS OF THE WORLD
Information and content.

mosaicaday.com - MOSAICA DAY
Dinner with friends.

myjewishlearning.com
MY JEWISH LEARNING

religioustolerance.org
RELIGIOUS TOLERANCE

skirball.com - THE SKIRBALL CULTURAL CENTER IN LOS ANGELES

sojos.net- SOJOURNERS
An activist progressive Christian ministry.

swirlinc.org - SWIRL
A nonprofit organization for the mixed community.

ujc.org - UNITED JEWISH COMMUNITIES

universist.org
THE UN-RELIGION RELIGION FOR THE FAITHFULLY FAITHLESS

SHOPAHOLUKKAH

3rliving.com
Eco-friendly ornaments.

alefjudaica.com
Supplier of Judaica giftware.

bamboulaltd.com
Handcrafted ornaments from Africa.

bethanylowe.com
Vintage style Christmas décor.

bethmallonphotography.com
Dog photography and gifts.

bodhitoys.com
Dog toys for the enlightened pup.

byerschoice.com
Menorah and Christmas tree advent calendars.

cafepress.com/chrismukkah
Chrismukkah ornaments, T-shirts and gift items.

chocolategelt.com
Hanukkah gelt in all sizes and permutations.

chosencouture.com
Featuring an eclectic assortment of nontraditional Jewish gifts.

chrismukkah.com
Chrismukkah greeting cards, books and gifts.

christmascovedesigns.com
Hand-knit Chrismukkah stockings.

christopherradko.com
Jewish star and menorah ornaments.

copajudaica
The "December Dilemma," Chewish dog toys and whimsical Judaica.

creativecandles.com
Holiday candles.

eieiostudio.com
Groovy gift wrap.

elope.com
Festive hybrid holiday hats.

fancyflours.com
Specialty baking supplies and edible sugar whimsies.

fantasiawear.com
Mrs. Santa Claus attire

frenchbull.com
Colorful Melamine dinnerware.

georgesf.com
Accouterments for dogs and cats.

groovyholidays.com
Fun and groovy holiday bags.

heroicproductions.com
Judah Maccabee plush doll.

jewishmusicgroup.com
Lots of music on CD.

judaicaspecialties.com
Everything you'll need for a merry Hanukkah.

laluzcandles.com
Soy-based holiday candles.

latkelarry.com
Toy doll.

koolkipah.com
Yarmulkes and kippahs.

manischewitz.com
Kosher products.

mayadeviimports.com
Ethnic ornaments from India and Africa.

menorah.com
Menorahs and Hanukkah accessories.

miaonline.com
Glass ornaments from Poland.

michelleganttceramics.com
Ceramic bowls, mugs and vessels.

nobleworksinc.com
Christmas and Chrismukkah greeting cards.

oldenglishcrackers.com
Traditional English Christmas crackers.

onelifepoducts.net
Hanukkah tree topper.

originalsbygwen.com
Hybrid holiday stockings.

oytotheworld.com
"Oy to the World" CD.

partypartnersdesign.com
Vintage paper fancies.

recycledplanetstore.com
Ornaments, trees, wreaths made from recycled plastic.

schylling.com
Vintage style tin toys.

shmaltz.com
Brewers of He'Brew Beer.

tesoros.com
Mexican folk art and Frida Kahlo candles.

tibetcollection.com
Tibet Collection of artifacts and prayer flags.

theocInsider.com
Yarmuclaus hat

trixieandpeanut.com
Dogmatic fetching and kvetching

unionwear.com
Custom yarmulkes.

urbanoutfitters.com
Cool holiday gifts.

whitehousechristmas.com
Separation of church and state ornaments.

yarmulkebra.com
Makers of the Yarmulke Bra.

yayodesigns.inc
Gnome and fawn lights.

zaros.com
Baker of New York's best black-and-white cookie.

zeigerenterprises
Russian nesting dolls.

Obligations & Guilty Acknowledgments

Mazel tov to the merry mishpocha who enriched *Chrismukkah* beyond my imagination: Ann Treistman, my editor, a born mish-masher who helped me sort the mish from the mash; Michael Jacobs and David Rosen, for believing in this fakakta project; Tumbleweed Design Studio, for wrapping it all up in one beautiful package; Larry Stanley, for the steady focus and enthusiasm; Kathy Stark, an extraordinary chef who purees ideas into delicious reality; Rachel Pearson, *Chrismukkah*'s awesome illustrator and honorary Jewish princess; Edna Kaplan and Phyllis Laorenza Linnehan, the mish-mash dynamic duo of PR; Allan Secher, for blessing Montana with one cool rabbi; Karen Frank, who kept me kosher with the law; John, Nadine, Kim, Randy, Jean and the entire Gantt family, for teaching me the true meaning of Christmas; Rod Shapiro, my main mensch; Starky's Authentic, the only place in Montana to get a decent bowl of matzo ball soup; Chadz "I'm not your Shlepping Stone" Café in Livingston; Lynn "Oy Joy" Gordon, "Are there fifty-two ways to say thanks?"; Jody Rein and David Borgenicht, my early instigators; Dan "Bubbie and Zayde" Bloom in Taiwan and cousins Mark, Daniele, Julian and Zach Gompertz, for the bagels and lox. Chrismukkah kudos to the Jewish Museum of Berlin, Michael Nathanson, Seth Cohen, Sara Schwimmer Ned Rosenbaum, Daniel Klein and Freke Vuijst. Finally, thanks to all the anonymous, unacknowledged posters of jokes, parody songs and obscure trivia on the web whose work was an inspiration.

PHOTO CREDITS

PROJECT MANAGER: **DAVID ROSEN**
EDITOR: **ANN TREISTMAN**
DESIGNER: **TUMBLEWEED**
PRODUCTION MANAGER: **KIM TYNER**

LIBRARY OF CONGRESS CATALOGING-IN-PUBLICATION DATA:GOMPERTZ, RON.

CHRISMUKKAH : EVERYTHING YOU NEED TO KNOW TO CELEBRATE THE HYBRID

HOLIDAY / RON GOMPERTZ.

P. CM.

ISBN-13: 978-1-58479-558-2

ISBN-10: 1-58479-558-1

1. CHRISTMAS. 2. HANUKKAH. 3. CHRISTIANITY AND OTHER RELIGIONS–JUDAISM. 4. JUDAISM—RELATIONS—CHRISTIANITY.
I. TITLE.

BV45.G66 2006

263'.915–DC22

2006011559

PUBLISHED IN 2006 BY STEWART, TABORI & CHANG AN IMPRINT OF HARRY N. ABRAMS, INC.

THE TEXT OF THIS BOOK WAS COMPOSED IN:
FRANKLIN GOTHIC, BLOCK BERTHOLD, LO-TYPE, BRODY D, DOLMEN & GOUDY HEAVYFACE

PRINTED AND BOUND IN MEXICO

10 9 8 7 6 5 4 3 2 1

HNA

harry n. abrams, inc.
a subsidiary of La Martinière Groupe

115 WEST 18TH STREET
NEW YORK, NY 10011
WWW.HNABOOKS.COM

ABOUT THE AUTHOR

RON GOMPERTZ is a native of New York City and son of German-Jewish refugees. His father, a semi-famous designer known as "Mr. Fred," would shlep the author along to private fittings with Barbra Streisand and other Go-Go era celebrity clientele. His mother used to illustrate greeting cards. Ron's checkered past provides proof of ongoing ADD. His career included stints as the "Good Humor" man, downhill ski racer, Bloomingdale's pots and pans buyer, Godzilla toy expert, alchemist, mosaicist, record producer, virtual-reality huckster, general contractor, and most recently, inventor of hoax holidays. He met his wife, Michelle, a ceramic artist and Web designer while computer dating. They have a daughter, Minna, and live in Montana, near Yellowstone National Park, where Ron spends most of his time keeping track of naughty and nice people who send e-mail to Chrismukkah.com.

ABOUT THE CONTRIBUTORS

KATHY STARK, *Chrismukkah*'s chef, is a culinary instructor and professional food writer with a passion for collecting vintage recipes and cookbooks. Kathy recently relocated with her husband, Glen, and their two children from Detroit to Bozeman. After leaving her longtime position as executive chef with the Honeybaked Ham Company, Kathy and Glen opened Starky's Authentic—Montana's only real Jewish delicatessen serving homemade matzo ball soup daily.

LARRY STANLEY, *Chrismukkah*'s photographer, is a native of Kansas City, Missouri. Larry has traveled a circuitous route, studying and traveling through Australia, China and Tibet. Larry makes his home in Livingston, Montana—specializing in product and portrait photography. He was the staff photographer on the PBS series *Frontier House* and his work has appeared in *TV Guide, Woman's World, Lucky*, books by Harper Collins, and Conde Nast Publishing.

RACHEL PEARSON, *Chrismukkah*'s illustrator, received her degree in psychology from the University of California and a BFA from the California College of Arts and Crafts (CCAC). As principal of RDP Studio, she has designed countless logos, CD covers and Web sites, but is best known for her eccentric character illustrations—"The Pathological Optimist," the soon-to-be-published "Luciland" and a line of organic baby apparel called "Speesees." Rachel is also a talented singer, dancer and vaulter.